Deleuze & Collaborative Writing

COMPLICATED

CONVERSATION

A Book Series of Curriculum Studies

William F. Pinar
General Editor

VOLUME 38

The Complicated Conversation series is part of the Peter Lang Education list.
Every volume is peer reviewed and meets
the highest quality standards for content and production.

PETER LANG
New York • Washington, D.C./Baltimore • Bern
Frankfurt • Berlin • Brussels • Vienna • Oxford

Jonathan Wyatt, Ken Gale,
Susanne Gannon, Bronwyn Davies

Deleuze & Collaborative Writing

AN IMMANENT PLANE OF COMPOSITION

PETER LANG
New York • Washington, D.C./Baltimore • Bern
Frankfurt • Berlin • Brussels • Vienna • Oxford

Library of Congress Cataloging-in-Publication Data

Deleuze and collaborative writing: an immanent plane of composition /
Jonathan Wyatt, Ken Gale, Susanne Gannon, Bronwyn Davies.
p. cm. — (Complicated conversation: a book series of curriculum studies; v. 38)
Includes bibliographical references and index.
1. Authorship—Collaboration. 2. Authorship—Philosophy.
3. Deleuze, Gilles, 1925–1995. I. Wyatt, Jonathan. II. Gale, Ken.
III. Gannon, Susanne. IV. Davies, Bronwyn.
PN145.D43   808'.02—dc22   2010046073
ISBN 978-1-4331-1319-2 (hardcover)
ISBN 978-1-4331-1318-5 (paperback)
ISSN 1534-2816

Bibliographic information published by **Die Deutsche Nationalbibliothek**.
Die Deutsche Nationalbibliothek lists this publication in the "Deutsche
Nationalbibliografie"; detailed bibliographic data is available
on the Internet at http://dnb.d-nb.de/.

Cover image: River Thames, Folly Bridge, Oxford, UK. Photograph by Tessa Wyatt.

The paper in this book meets the guidelines for permanence and durability
of the Committee on Production Guidelines for Book Longevity
of the Council of Library Resources.

Contents

Acknowledgments

Ken and Jonathan thank Norman Denzin for the invitation to form the original panel on Deleuze and collaborative writing at the 2009 International Congress of Qualitative Inquiry, and Bronwyn and Susanne for being up for participating. Thanks too, as ever, to Jane Speedy for her effervescent encouragement. Ken thanks his lovely children Katy, Reuben and Phoebe, whose presence in his life is so much a part of him whenever he writes; and his colleagues and students in the Faculty of Education at the University of Plymouth for their interest in and support for his work. He thanks Jonathan, too, for the sincere, unstinting and invaluable friendship that he has shared with him throughout their writing together. Jonathan thanks Tessa, Joe and Holly for the ways in which they have variously provided inspiration for, tolerated and challenged him through the writing of this book. To Bronwyn, Ken, and Susanne, he says: thank you for this experience, which has been truly fascinating.

Bronwyn thanks Jonathan and Tessa for their warm hospitality, support and friendship, and Ken for his generous hospitality and the sharing of his wonderful Cornish landscape. Thanks too to Viv for the moment by the Cornish sea when the sun was going down and lighting up the universe. Thanks too to those in Maynooth in Ireland with their love of stories. And to Susanne, for being such a wonderful colleague and friend, always. Thanks too, to Bristol University for the award of the Benjamin Meaker visiting professorship in March and April of 2010, which provided the time and place to work on this manuscript. She would particularly like to thank all those in Bristol who were such inspiring collegial companions and friends during the period of this writing; to Jane Speedy and Artemi Sakelleriadis in particular she offers her thanks. To her sons she offers very special thanks, for being there, and for their forbearance and love. The responses that Jake and Dan offered to the story of their father were deeply moving, and significant in helping her to allow that story to unfold. To Jonathan, my deepest gratitude for being there on the ethics plateau.

Susanne thanks Jonathan and Ken for the initial invitation to partic-ipate, and Norman Denzin for invitations before and after that that have given impetus to this work, and for publishing an earlier version of the text that appears here as Plateau One in the *International Review of Qualitative Research*. A special thank you to all the people who helped us invoke the spirit of Deleuze at that early morning session at ICQI 2009. Thanks to Jonathan, Ken and Bronwyn who kept surprising and delighting her from various far aways, as she was tethered to more tedious aspects of academic life. She continues to read and write her way hesitantly through the big hessian sack of Deleuze, a task which has been intensely pleasurable in the company of J, K and B.

As the "JKSB" assemblage we collectively acknowledge that what we each became in the writing was only made possible by the collective presence of the others.

Beginning (JKSB)

In which we tell the reader how we four, the assemblage we have come to know as JKSB, came to write this book. We introduce some of the methodic (and non-methodic) practices we have taken up throughout the book, and open up the multiple space of Deleuzian concepts that we work and play with in this extended exploration of collaborative writing.

This book is an engagement with Gilles Deleuze and collaborative writing. We ask here: how might we think of collaborative writing if we think with the concepts that Deleuze has generated? And, how might we begin to write, together, on what Deleuze would call *an immanent plane of composition*? On such a Deleuzian plane, or plateau, it was not appropriate to make Deleuze external to us, as if he were the authority who might inform us on the correct way forward. Instead we sought to make Deleuze one of us, and to open up, with him, a new stream of thought, and of being, in order to explore our topic of Deleuze and collaborative writing.

So why an immanent plane of composition? Immanence derives from the Latin, meaning "to remain within." In Deleuzian philosophy this does not mean within the bounded individual self, but *within* life; not just human life, but all life, organic and inorganic, which Deleuze refers to as Being. Deleuzian immanence indicates a conceptual space in which one seeks to dissolve all binaries, and the categorizations that divide one from another; and to locate the Divine in all things. On this immanent plane God and matter are not separable, any more than mind and body, interior and exterior, self and other, theory and practice, man and animal, organic and inorganic. The question is never this *or* that, but always this *and* that. "Or" becomes "and" in what Deleuze called stuttering: and and and. Deleuze struggled to find a way of bringing together this idea that we are all part of the same Being, *and at the same time,* that we are multiple and emergent. In opposing binary thought and categorisation, he was not interested in making us all the same, but in finding how to think the multiple singularities within what he called the One-All: "A single and same voice for the whole thousand-voiced multiple, a single and same Ocean for all the drops, a single clamour of Being for all beings" (Deleuze, 1994: 304).

On the immanent plane of composition we are all part of the same Being and, at the same time, the interesting aspect, the creative life-giving aspect, does not lie in sameness but in divergence. Deleuze drew from the creative evolution that Bergson (1998) had mapped out in 1910, where creative affirmations lie in new experiences, through which the not-yet-known, the not-yet-imagined, can unfold—can be composed. Divergence is not to be thought as a feature of the individual of phenomenology, whose conscious intentions lie at the centre of a somewhat narcissistic, bounded ego (Davies, 2010a). Deleuze is interested in multiplicity, not of multiple identities, but in an "ontology [that] merges with the univocity of Being" (Deleuze, 2004c: 179), where univocity is the creative voice of matter.

Deleuze does not thus seek to populate the world with anarchic, sovereign individuals, whose will or choice is paramount, as many have thought. His concept of the automaton, for example, "strictly precludes any idea of ourselves as being, at any time, the source of what we think or do. Everything always stems from afar—indeed, everything is always "already-there," in the infinite and inhuman resource of the One" (Badiou, 2000: 12). Thinking and being on a plane of immanence in the Deleuzian sense is not a celebration of the autonomous individual of phenomenology, but rather, it "requires that you place yourself where thought has already started, as close as possible to a singular case and to the movement of thought. Thinking happens "behind your back" and you are impelled and constrained by it" (Badiou, 2000: 14).

Our challenge, then, in writing on an immanent plane of composition with Deleuze, has been to find our own way of mobilizing this resource of the One, of thinking and being where thought has already started—in this case thought about Deleuze and collaborative writing. But unlike Deleuze, who, as philosopher, could identify the multiplication of concepts as his way of approaching the problem of infinite divergence and creative evolution, we, as social scientists and educators, must find our own way of engaging in thought, and our own way of engaging in being, that opens up the not-yet-known within itself. We must work with experience, multiplying it, while also drawing on, or, more correctly, playing with Deleuze's multiplicity of concepts.

But working with experience opens up significant challenges in this Deleuzian framework. Experience is interesting to Deleuze, but not in the ways we generally think of in the social sciences, where accounts of experience operate as windows onto particular individuals or their social worlds (Davies and Davies, 2007). He asks us to think of experience as interesting insofar as it is a manifestation of emergent being, where subjects come to exist, unfold, as virtual points of intersection among concepts, percepts and affects. Experience opens a fold of Being, a fold that can be refolded and unfolded. Each fold is a mode of being that both envelops and is enveloped in the One-All of Being.

Deleuze does not deny the existence of individuals and their experience; they are ontologically real. But their engagement in being, in univocal being, in all its complexity and divergence, opens up not the usual question who are you in particular (what is your identity that I might judge you and thereby judge myself), but *how is this possible?* Deleuze asks, in relation to experience, "how is that possible? How is this possible in an internal way? [Engaging with someone's experience] you relate the thing or the statement to the mode of existence that it implies, that it envelops in itself. How must it be in order to say that? Which manner of Being does this imply?" (Deleuze, 1980: np). How might I comprehend

Being in new ways through listening to you inside the fold of your experience?

In order to explore collaborative writing *with* Deleuze, and with his concepts at play, it was not appropriate to make a plan in order to impose what we already knew on the task. We asked instead what mode or manner of being might be made possible within the space of writing to and with each other, and with Deleuze. We thus sought to open up a theory and practice of collaborative writing, experimenting with what it might be from within itself. For Deleuze, being and knowing are the same thing: "it is the same thing which occurs and is said" (2004: 206); we could come to know collaborative writing by doing it; we could do something by knowing it from inside itself.

Two of us (Jonathan and Ken in the UK) had been writing together on a collaborative doctorate, and had drawn on the collective biography methodology that another two of us (Bronwyn and Susanne in Australia) had developed (Davies and Gannon 2006 and 2009). Responding to a suggestion from Norman Denzin, that the JK assemblage extend itself into the field of Deleuze and collaborative writing for the purposes of presenting a symposium at the 2009 International Congress of Qualitative Inquiry (QI), JK reassembled themselves with Bronwyn and Susanne to become *the JKSB Deleuze and collaborative writing assemblage—JKSB for short.*

The JK Assemblage

Ken began with an attempt to collect thoughts and senses together in order to make an account of what the JK assemblage had been, and hence what the JKSB assemblage might be . . .

I have been trying to collect my thoughts and feelings about the way in which I see Deleuze influencing the collective biography work that I have been doing these past few years. The collection that is tumbling around in my senses at the moment is an interesting and exciting assemblage and I am not going to attempt an orderly unravelling; I am going to see what threads and fibres begin to reveal themselves as I stutter in my own language and the (minor) language I hope that I will be able to use with Bronwyn, Jonathan and Suzanne.

Collective biography: Jonathan and I didn't call it that when we started. This is how we described what we thought we were doing in our collaborative writing in the early pages of our dissertation (Gale and Wyatt, 2008c: 7):

> When we originally decided to write together, as students on the doctoral programme at Bristol, we were motivated to enquire into our different writing styles....In our first writing (Gale and Wyatt, 2006, 2007) we reflect upon these different writing styles: on the one hand there was Ken, the serious-minded, inquisitive thinker, engaged in conceptual analysis, eager to inquire and to present ideas in a dense and detailed "academic" style; and, on the other, we found Jonathan, the storyteller, exploring the subtleties and nuances of the heart through narrative accounts of loss.

This interest in styles was our first intersection, the point at which desire was sparked, a desire that soon pushed, pulled, teased and taunted our writing in different directions. As we began to write with and to each other we began to be aware that we were writing in a different way.

Since beginning this work together much has changed from the simple binary account of identity and style that we offered then. Our becomings have overlapped. Similar to St. Pierre we have become interested in "Keeping subjectivity in play, mobile, a line of flight with no referent and no destination as our desire and our ethical charge...subjectivity is a mobile assemblage that arranges and rearranges itself outside all totalising paranoia" (1997: 413).

We have discovered, and begun to use in different ways, important and, what we consider to be, connected, or perhaps related, methodologies. So we will continue to explore the ways in which Laurel Richardson's (2000) "writing as a method of inquiry" continues to infuse our writing and enthuse us in so many ways in the writing we undertake with each other. We feel that we have taken Richardson's method of inquiry into a collective domain. We continually sense the presence of Braidotti (1994) in what we do; we continue to become "nomadic subjects" as we move through the spaces that we both create and inhabit.

Opening Up the Collaborative JKSB Space

Following Ken's opening, we began by writing to each other through emails. We wrote into the space of the four of us, no longer "ourselves" in our difference from each other, or even in our sameness, but intensities of being as they were called up by that space and the spaces around us, and by our play with an array of Deleuzian concepts. The intensities we wrote about, what Deleuze might also call *events*, sought the actuality of collaborative writing through the infinite virtuality of moments of being within the collaborative space we opened up. We wrote about moments of being, or what Deleuze calls *haecceities*, as these moments, these movements, became possible in this space between/among us. Haecceities, in Halsey's (2007: 125–6) words:

> make no distinction between centre and periphery, inside and outside, subject and object and, therefore, humans and nature... A haecceity is a moment of pure speed and intensity (an individuation)—like when a swimming body becomes-wave and is momentarily suspended in nothing but an intensity of forces and rhythms. Or like when body becomes-horizon such that it feels only the interplay between curves and surfaces and knows nothing of here and there, observer and observed.

Deleuze was a significant presence in our conversations, giving us the conceptual impulse to enable us to become, at one and the same time, ontologically present to ourselves and each other, and, at least some of the time, no longer separate identities with boundaries to be managed and defended. Deleuze emphasises, when he talks about his own collaborative writing, that what flowed between him and his collaborator was best conceived as movement, as event, rather than as meetings or exchanges between individuals with specific attributes:

> Félix and I, and many others like us, don't feel we're persons exactly. Our individuality is rather that of events, which isn't making any grand claim, given that haecceities can be modest and microscopic. I've tried in all my books to discover the nature of events; it's a philosophical concept, the only one capable of ousting the verb "to be" and attributes. From this viewpoint, writing with someone else becomes completely natural. It's just a question of something passing through you, a current, which alone has a proper name. Even when you think you're writing on your own, you're always doing it with someone else you can't always name. (Deleuze, 1995: 141)

In our emails to each other we documented the many microscopic haecceities, the flow of events in the space between or among us, the intensities of our being-in-relation as collaborative writers. We constructed out of the flow of conversation among us, a play, which we presented at QI, with each of us appearing as a "presence," and with Deleuze as our fifth "presence." That play appears here in a modified form as our first plateau: *A play on and with Deleuze and collaborative writing*. It mobilises Deleuzian thought to provide a means of looking at collaborative writing as performativity, as a means of becoming, each in the space made possible by the listening presence of the others. It works as an introduction to Deleuzian thought, and to the space in-between the five of us that opened up in this work. We delved into and extended Deleuze and Guattari's "between the twos," though for us it was between/among the five—Jonathan, Ken, Susanne, Bronwyn, and Gilles. In that first writing and performance, we elaborated this idea of the in-between, looking at how we wrote our selves for our collaborative others, these intimate strangers, in deeply embodied ways. The words that flowed in between and among the four of us sent out ripples that became manifest, both in our writing, and in each of our everyday lives. We extended this discussion of flow and the in-between with discussions (or Acts) on haecceities, on listening and on writing. These themes seemed to lie at the heart of our exchanges with one another and what we understood and practiced as collaborative writing.

In this book we extend the lines of inquiry that the play opened up, presenting them as a series of Plateaus. Our methodology can be described as a fertile encounter between collective biography as developed by Bronwyn and Susanne (Davies and Gannon, 2006, 2009) and nomadic inquiry as developed by Jonathan and Ken (Gale and Wyatt, 2009). In both of these methodologies the researchers are their own subjects, though the identity of those subjects is not the object of the inquiry. We briefly elaborate here each of these approaches to research, since they open up ways of thinking about research that are quite different from what Deleuze (and our readers) might imagine doing. We then discuss why we have called each shift in our writing another plateau rather than a chapter.

Collective Biography

Collective biography is a research strategy that works with memory, and with the virtual body that memory evokes. Memory is not treated here as fixed or real; there is, as Bergson (1998) points out, no drawer in the brain that stores a veridical past. The memories are of virtual rather than actual events, and each time they are accessed they are re-made in their virtual intensities. Collective biography, as a set of research practices, engages in a movement away from individualized, liberal-humanist versions of the subject, toward a poststructural conception of the subject—a subject-in-relation, in-process (Davies and Gannon, 2006, 2009, Davies 2010a).

The practice of collective biography generally involves the researchers (who are their own subjects) meeting over several consecutive days, at first talking and reading about their chosen topic (which might include topics such as subjectification, agency, power, bullying, recognition—each time, a topic the group of researchers have chosen as relevant to their research interests). In response to trigger questions such as, for example, what is your first memory of not being recognised, participants tell their own remembered stories evoked by the questions. Each participant listens to the others' telling, questioning where the words are not clear, listening in order to know how this story is lived in an internal way, questioning the story-teller when, as listener, they find they cannot imagine what happened. Each listens and questions, and listens again, in order to know the memory for themselves, in its specific embodied, affective detail.

The trajectory that each story maps on to in this telling and open listening, is one that moves away from "this is my autobiography," toward opening up a space of univocity, where univocity is the creative voice of matter.

When each person has told one or more memories, and each one has been openly listened to by the others, each participant writes her or his memories, paying particular attention to both the affect, the body before language, *and* to the words themselves. The written stories focus on one pivotal moment, attempting to capture the haecceity, or just-thisness of that particular moment. They are written from within the folds of one's own body, without clichés and explanations, and without judgement. They do not import expressions that would be foreign to the subjects in the stories, that would draw attention to the story-teller now, or take attention away from the haecceity of this remembered moment.

Each story is then read out loud to the group. The participants listen again, openly and with care, to the affect, but also focussing on the words, listening again in order to know the story from inside itself, to register it in the folds of their own listening bodies. Each one asks, in listening, "how is this possible in an internal way," listening in order to know for themselves "the mode of existence that it implies, that it envelops in itself" (Deleuze, 1980: np). When they can't enter the story at any point, and can't come to know it in this way, they make a note of where the words did not open up a space they could imagine, and the story is discussed in light of these blank spots. The flow of talk back and forth around, and inside, each story further enables the story-teller to know and write the detail of his or her story in an embodied way, and at the same time to open up for the listeners the detail of the story that allows them too to know it, internally, for themselves. In this flow back and forth, the listeners offer insights from their own take-up of the story as it resonates in their bodies, asking *is this how it was?*

Sometimes the listeners tell some of their own memories as a way of opening up a different entry point to another's remembered moment-of-being that they cannot find the way into. They ask, *does this memory of mine, in its difference, help us to tease out this moment, so that we can, in our collective listening, know it internally?* This exchange of bodily sensations and intensities creates a double movement in which each story-teller knows their story differently, registering the multiple intensities, their own and others', that make this moment live. Each listener in registering those multiple intensities, now closely linked and overlapping with their own intensities, their own memories, has become someone other than themselves, whose co-implication in the lives of others has become visible.

Following this reading and open listening, each story is re-written, and read out loud again to the others, who listen again, registering again the thisness of Being. In this listening, each is open and vulnerable to the other (Davies, 2010b). Thought and being emerge in such moments of Being, creatively, becoming different in that moment, that movement. It is an ongoing process, a movement, a coming to know and to be differently from how one knew and was at the beginning.

The story-tellers finally turn back to the topic in relation to which the stories were generated, and asks how these stories might contribute to new thought about the topic being addressed by the stories. A paper, or series of papers, is then collaboratively developed, working with the insights that have emerged through the process of memory-work. This stage of collaborative writing may well be the place where further shifts in thought are accomplished.

Collective biography was inspired in the first place by Haug et al.'s (1987) memory-work. Memory-work involves the writing and subsequent analysis of remembered stories that researchers can collectively use to generate their own critique of theory. Their analyses, which begin with their own stories, are aimed at discovering the constitutive means by which they had formed themselves into personalities, focusing on "the way individuals continuously reproduce society as a whole: the way they enter into pre-given structures, within which they reproduce both themselves, and the categories of society" (Haug et al. 1987: 40). In particular:

> What we required of ourselves was that we consider and investigate both the production of a specifically feminine sexuality and, alongside this, the constitution of the sexual itself as a process that produces the insertion of women into, and their subordination within, determinate social practices….[We have used] our own memories [as] the empirical element of our research….Indeed memory-work is only possible if the subject and object of research are one and the same person. Even notions of "subject" and "object" had to be problematized in our work, amongst other reasons because they posit both as fixed and knowable entities, neither of which is subject to change. (Haug et al. 1987: 33–35)

In Bronwyn's development of collective biography (Davies, 1994, 2000a) she took up this same dual strategy of retrieving memories and using those memories to explore the processes of subjectification (Davies et al. 2001). But collective biography differs from memory work in that Haug et al.'s work, while interested in "society," works from the point of view of the individualized subject. They are interested in the "therapeutic outcomes" of their work, outcomes that might give individuals a greater capacity to resist oppressive versions of femininity and of the Marxist theory that dominated at the time of their writing. Collective biography, in contrast, works *with* poststructuralist theory and against the grain of phenomenology's liberal-humanist subject. Similar to Haug et al. it makes visible, and therefore revisable, the every day discourses through which we make meanings and selves; but collective biography deconstructs phenomenology's individual, the individual that is thought to exist independent of various collectives, of discourse, of history, of time and place (Davies, 2000a, 2000b). The primary focus is not so much therapeutic, but is on generating *savoir*, thinking in order to know differently, and in the process, being modified through what one comes to know (Foucault, 2000). It is about generating the means to see how we become subjects, and go on becoming subjects, how we are generated within, and generate, what Deleuze calls the clamour of Being, the "single and same voice for the whole thousand-voiced multiple, a single and same Ocean for all the drops, a single clamour of Being for all beings" (Deleuze, 1994: 304).

In our book, *Doing Collective Biography* (2006), Bronwyn and Susanne coined the term mo(ve)ment in order to evoke the doubled action involved in our collective story-telling and writing, of dwelling in and on particular moments of being, and of movement toward, or openness to, new possibilities both of seeing and of being. In telling, listening, questioning, writing, reading and rewriting our stories, a shift takes place. The memories are no longer told and heard as just autobiographical (that is, an assemblage of already known stories that mark one individualized person off from the next), but as opening up for, and in, each other, knowledges of being that previously belonged only to the other, as that other's (often illegible) marks of identity. In working collectively with memories, we live intimately within our own bodies, and our bodies take on the intimate knowledge of each other's being. Each subject's specificity in its very particularity, in its sensory detail, becomes, through this process, the collectively imagined detail through which we know ourselves as human, even as more human—as humans-in-relation, humans who are immersed in and emerge from the clamor of Being.

Although collective biography workshops are usually conducted in this intensive manner, it is important that collective biography remains open and responsive to the specific context, the participants, and the creative possibilities that the particular research question might generate.

In the context of this project on Deleuze and collaborative writing, our location in different hemispheres required a radical break with usual practices. The engagement with JK's nomadic writing and with Deleuze, meant that collective biography morphed in entirely new ways.

Nomadic Inquiry

Nomadic inquiry seeks the liminal space in which difference emerges, in which writer and reader no longer know themselves or the other in the same way. Jane Speedy recently reflected on the beginning of the JK assemblage from her position as doctoral supervisor:

> [J and K were] Nomads moving in space time consciousness, following lines of flight, unsure of direction and indulging in the pressure of the force fields of uncertainty.
>
> I was off with two nomads, or, at least, they were off and I was watching from an open door. I was standing on the threshold and could see both ways—down the dark corridors behind, lined with shelves of scholarly texts and manuscripts, and out into the sand and wind beyond—brightly lit, but hazy and uncharted.
>
> Dust storms. I anticipated dust storms from the outset. (Gale, Speedy and Wyatt, 2010: 23)

As the becomings of their doctoral journey took on an intensity that they had not anticipated, as the challenge to their individuating selves increased, and their separate subjectivities began to come undone, Jane's supervisory presence slowly and inexorably mutated, from a somewhat detached but nevertheless curious voyeur, to one of fully engaged collaborator. Bronwyn also found this movement in her own reading of the completed dissertation: "I found myself, as reader, drawn into the folds and plateaus of their relationality, first as an outsider looking in, curious about what it was they were allowing me to see, then slowly taking up the *space-in-between* that was generated in their writing" (Davies, 2009: vii).

Jonathan and Ken's nomadic collaborative writing drew on collective biography (see also Gale and Wyatt, 2008b), on writing as a method of inquiry (Richardson and St. Pierre, 2005); on poetic representation

(Richardson, 1997; Gannon, 2004) and on autoethnography (Ellis, 2004; Gannon, 2006). This was an experiment in writing, in using these practices to explore what else might open out in a nomadic Deleuzian space. Nomadic inquiry, as they experimented with it, involved crystalline territorialisations in and around various points. Haecceities emerged through the creative evolution of the interior in relation to the exterior. Change did not follow an underlying logos based on transcendent principles, but was constant and always-in-relation to other changes.

The Deleuzian figure of the rhizome provides one possible image of nomad space:

> ...unlike trees or their roots, the rhizome connects any point to any other point, and its traits are not necessarily linked to traits of the same nature...It is composed not of units but of dimensions, or rather directions in motion. It has neither beginning nor end, but always a middle (milieu) from which it grows and which it overspills...(it) operates by variation, expansion, conquest, capture, offshoot...it has multiple entryways and its own lines of flight. (Deleuze and Guattari, 2004b: 23)

"The notion of the rhizome is Deleuze's leading figuration: it points to a redefinition of the activity of philosophy as the quest for new images of thought, better suited to a nomadic, disjunctive self" (Braidotti, 1994: 165). Nomadic space can thus, in part, be characterised in this rhizomatic way. But it is also imagined by Deleuze as lines of flight taking off from the sedimented order of the already known, in new directions, plotting different courses, and engaging in experimentation. Rhizomes and lines of flight offer escape from closed formations and connect with other multiplicities from the outside. They resist the establishment of fixed orders or systems and rigid structural configurations.

Nomadic writing is transgressive, it brings together affect and percept, it is a mutating, shifting, creative process of conceptualisation. It challenges the traditional humanistic and phenomenological constructions of spatial and temporal selves. As Braidotti (1994: 165) says of Deleuzian thought:

> thinking cannot and must not be reduced to reactive (Deleuze says "sedentary") critique. Thinking can be critical if by critical we mean the active, assertive

process of inventing new images of thought...thinking is about finding new images. Thinking is about change and transformation.

In contrast, there are spaces that have been territorialised, laid down inside lines, or striations, that do not allow new thought to emerge. Deleuze envisaged the space in between territories, or subjects, as a fertile space. By envisioning their own landscapes in Deleuzian ways, as territories, Jonathan and Ken's newly emerging and constantly shifting nomadic subjectivity began to evolve creatively in a space or spaces between-the-two. In their growing familiarity with and immersion in a Deleuzian "logic of sense" (2004c) the categorical difference between "territories" became increasingly displaced by the differentiating affects and percepts of "territorialisation."

Ken noticed how his reading of various books and journals in his collaborative thesis writing with Jonathan was becoming multiple, volatile and highly charged with a nomadic literacy of self and other. The image of the artist Francis Bacon pacing up and down in, what he referred to as the "compost," the impenetrable and ever changing clutter of his Reece Mews studio floor, continued to remain significant for Ken as his immersion in, and lines of flight from, this nomadic space continued (Peppiatt, 2008). With Bachelard (1969) he began to experience a "poetics of space" in which a growing aesthetic and evaluative sense of the intimacy of this *between-the-two* was taking him further, and with a certain delirious sense of joy, into a world of the not-yet-known—into what Deleuze calls smooth space. And as Deleuze says: "(T)here is a significant difference between the spaces: sedentary space is striated, by walls, enclosures, and roads between enclosures, while nomad space is smooth, marked only by "traits" that are effaced and displaced with the trajectory" (Deleuze and Guattari, 2004b: 381).

"In this *nomos*, this smooth space, lines of flight and escape occur, new relations are made in pulsing, vibrant and amorphous nomadic inquiries" (Gale and Wyatt, 2009: 43). It is *nomad space* rather than that of the *nomad* itself that is of significance here. Deleuze is at pains in his writing to move us away from thinking in terms of a romanticised notion of the individual that is somehow co-existent with being. This humanistic conception of a phenomenological subject is problematised by Deleuzian thought, which posits instead a world of pre-individual, impersonal singularities, and opens us up to the possibility of a volatile dynamism and openness, where "these singularities are mobile, they break in, thieving and stealing away, alternating back and forth, like anarchy crowned, inhabiting a nomad space" (Deleuze, 2004a: 143).

In this nomad space we are less likely to inquire into the categorical differences that, it might be claimed, exist between, say, men and women, man and animal, or between one species and another. Rather we are more likely to be curious about the intensities that might be seen to exist in the spaces that open up between these singularities. We are more likely to trouble the territorializations, the striations, the molar lines of force, through an acute appreciation of the nuances and flux of differenciations that might be present between and within them. A nomadic inquiry into subjectivity of this kind, places an emphasis on the becoming of the pre-individual, recognisable within processes of individuation, of leaning toward, hoping to open up, even momentarily, smooth space and within it, the not-yet-known.

Plateaus

We call the segments of writing in this book "plateaus" rather than "chapters." In *A Thousand Plateaus* (2004b: 24), Deleuze and Guattari stress that "a plateau is always in the middle, not at the beginning or the end. A rhizome is made of plateaus." Our plateaus are in homage to their work, and indicative of a movement toward rhizomatic thought. Rather than a book that constructs cumulative arguments and coherent conclusions, we wish to present a text that invites lines of flight between its sections, between its writers and between its readers, that opens toward settlements and understandings that are merely momentary and always provisional. Each plateau extends one of the many lines of flight that flew out in so many directions from the first work we four did together. These lines of flight fly across the segments of text and back and forth between them. They need not be read in the order in which they are placed in this text. They might be read at random, or perhaps some parts might not be read at all. In this sense the reader is also the author of the text. Deleuze and Guattari claim that they gave their book "a circular form, but only for laughs" (2004b: 24).

In his translator's foreword to *A Thousand Plateaus*, Massumi suggests that the reader "might follow each section to the plateau that rises from the smooth space of its composition, and…move from one plateau to the next at pleasure" (2004b: xv). This book has pleasure, and perhaps you might even find some laughs, but the plateaus that carried reverberations for us, that finally insisted on being written, that had the qualities for us of "continuous, self-vibrating region[s] of intensities" (Deleuze and Guattari, 2004b: 24) contain ambivalent and elaborate affects. We settle for now, in this book, in this present place and time of writing, on plateaus of the play, nightmares and the ontology of place, sea reflections, ethics, and collaborative writing.

The Blue Mountains west of Sydney, where Susanne lives, is a series of eucalyptus clad sandstone plateaus that from some lookouts seem to ripple all the way to the horizon. Escarpments and gorges cut into these plateaus, but can seem so close on some crisp autumn afternoons that you can imagine flinging a rope out from one to the other, or taking flight like a bird. It is most possible to see that these are plateaus once you are on them, in the middle of them, looking over their folds, peering into their gaps, and here too it seems that: "it's not easy to see things in the middle, rather than looking down on them from above or up at them from below, or from left to right or right to left: try it, you'll see that everything changes…never is a plateau separate from the cows that populate it, which are also the clouds in the sky" (Deleuze and Guattari, 2004b: 25). Look across and between our plateaus, stand on the escarpments if you will, fling out your own ropes, take flight.

The Present Work

Our written exchanges, through which we brought into being the JKSB assemblage, consisted of some detailed readings of Deleuze, combined with an intuitive leap into the not-yet-known of the space between and among us. Our communications were sometimes voluptuous, sometimes agonistic. In the *délire* of unexpected moments, in the call and response to one another, as we cast out lines that made new thought and being possible, we spun off the rails in different directions, leaving our-selves perhaps where we were at the beginning but somehow with everything transformed. *Délire* can't easily be translated. Joughin, Deleuze's translator (Deleuze, 1995: 186–187) writes that:

> Etymologically, *délirer* is to leave the furrow, go "off the rails," and wander in imagination and thought: meanings, images, and so on float in a dream logic rather than calmly following one another along the familiar lines or tracks of cold reason. But for Deleuze and Guattari solid "reason" and free floating *délire* are simply converse articulations of a single transformational "logic of sense."

Receiving writing from each other was not simply to be *touched* or even *moved*, but to have become other than oneself, no longer oneself, but a series of emergent flows and intensities. Deleuze reassures us that in such collaborations it is both remarkable but of no great concern how lit-tle authors might know about each other, how delicate their multiplic-ities and connections are, how oblique their references to their personal contexts might be, how indistinct, and yet how vividly seething their col-laborative "body-without-organs" (BwO) is.

The BwO is a concept Deleuze and Guattari generated to help de-couple us from our sense of ourselves bounded by our own skin, our egoic selves separated out from human, animal and earth others. The BwO as a concept sought to open up the idea of ourselves in relation, ourselves as co-extensive and co-implicated with the other. As Ken wrote into the JKSB space, about his work with Jonathan:

> It seems to me that our work together is both troubling and uplifting, some-times our work is affirmative and sometimes it takes us by surprise. We have claimed that our writing together on this plane of immanence can be likened to a "body-without-organs." Our work is not necessarily *organised* according to structure or function, within the context of principles of form or foundational values, rather we have found ourselves working to challenge regularities of form and content, we find ourselves de-territorialising striated spaces and fol-lowing lines of flight in the heady flow of nomadic inquiry.

To begin with we were tentative, emailing each other, unsure how to open up the space of our writing, not having made a plan that includ-ed organised turns or any other kind of ordering and orderly striation:

From Bronwyn, Firenze

Dear Sue, Ken and Jonathan

(Sue can you email this to Ken and Jonathan—navigating an Italian keyboard and screen, standing in the hotel lobby, is a nightmare) I have begun writing my reflections in response to Ken's opening reflections. Am on holiday for a week in Florence so at last had time to spare and have begun work on it. It is not finished yet by any means, but I'm wondering about sending it raw for feedback, to open up some more active collaboration. I've written about 6 pages one and a half space, and am inclined to think its better not to just have one say, but to send a shorter piece that then generates a reply and so on. What do you think? I'd have to get help attaching it but I think I could manage. I have got wireless connection with my own laptop, but the university made me take a new one away with me and it turns out to be a lemon and worse than useless. Let me know what you think. I can work on it for another week if that seems best, as I think there is more to say, and it will grow in its richness and complexity if I spend more time on it. Maybe it's just enough if you know it's coming. Let me know what you think

BRONWYN

From Susanne, in Sydney

Hi Ken and Jonathan—see message below from Bronwyn. I also started writing when I got back from the desert a week ago but it's brief and still a bit all over the place. [I wonder if I can claim that as a Deleuzian effect]. Bronwyn is grappling with the idiosyncrasies of international travel and work and I have been up to my neck in teaching and a book manuscript we are trying to finish off. What do you think of Bronwyn's idea of sending what we have even though it may yet not be totally finished? For me, I think the notion of sending a fully-crafted perfect piece that will be part of a beautifully elaborated and aesthetic collaboratively written text each time (as indeed your thesis is) is a little intimidating. I know (as you can tell) that when B and I began the correspondence that starts the chapter on collaborative writing in the book on collective biography it was fast and short and back and forth and in a crazy time of the year, yet it still said (maybe because it was less edited initially) what we wanted to say in quite a fresh and perhaps more personal way. And it has a certain energy that isn't always in other written work. I don't know how you two managed this tension between spontaneity of response (which some of Deleuze and Guattari's work seems to have too) with the care and caution with which we write much academic work. I know that even the most spontaneous work can be crafted and edited and shaped at a later time…That is how I like writing and believe it works…anyway these are early morning thoughts (while B is in Florence, I am in bed with the laptop—spring has come with rain and a cold snap and a convenient bout of insomnia). I guess the first leaves might be colouring where you are...

CIAO FROM US, SUE

From Ken, in Millbrook

I have just read Bronwyn and Susanne's e-mails and I am going to respond right away. Jonathan will endorse that I have a tendency to do this. I find myself becoming inspired, excited, angry, moved, whatever, by what I have just read and I feel that I have to respond. If you look at the chronology of our thesis you will see that often there is a small gap between J's writing to me and my writing back. Not always but quite frequently. I like what Deleuze says in *Dialogues* (Deleuze and Parnet, 2002) about his writing with Guattari, that they were never in step, or in tune, at the same time; their responses fluctuated according to where they were, who they were with and so on. I think the idea of sending you the thesis was just to set up a picture of where J and I have been so far. That's all!

I am happy to wing things off: I like that idea. For me this is the way that things ignite, burn and sometimes explode and in many ways offers some essence to collaborative writing. It doesn't have to be this way and often isn't but I also feel that this gives opportunities for fluidity, transgression and using writing as a method of inquiry. Sometimes I send things off, then wonder on reflection whether I should have done or not: it is the challenge to that rational thought that I like. I often subject myself to this kind of "reasoned" activity, which then pushes me into the affective domain of "worry," which then becomes an obstacle to action and nothing happens, nothing gets sent, communicated, whatever. So I tend to err on the side of "bashing it out," on taking a chance and worrying about it afterwards. Jonathan will tell you that if my co/respondents display slow response times in relation to something I have sent out I get frazzled, my paranoia kicks in and I revert to biting my nails!!

It feels to me this kind of spontaneous and therefore potentially transgressive approach offers all kinds of Deleuzian opportunities: it is likely to generate concepts as events; it is likely to trouble the striations of existing regulated space; it is there to encourage haecceities through its challenge to considered epistemological rigour; because of an affective presence there seems to be an opening into evaluative and aesthetic worlds that live with a Deleuzian logic of sense and offer opportunities to respond in multiple ways, through feeling, emotion, value, attitude as well as meaning...

Without wishing to advocate or admit descent into substance abuse (!) I really enjoyed Sadie Plant's book *Writing on Drugs* (1999). She offers great examples of the way in which writers through history have been "influenced" by various forms of intoxication but she also uses these examples in a way which, I think, offers an exciting reading of Deleuze and in particular his use of the Body without Organs. Reading this book opened up for me new and different terrains and really made me think about Deleuze and collaborative writing as a way that suggests that writing is just not "about," but that it can just "be." It suggests forms of trangressive writing, it challenges the form-content binary and the familiar tropes that support it, it opens up space for performative nomadic inquiry and also for a reflexive consideration of that. It also encourages me to write sometimes when I have had some wine or when I have come back from the pub!

OK! Just to say then that sometimes, I too like the "fast and short and back and forth" but that also I agree "that even the most spontaneous work can be crafted and edited and shaped at a later time"—I think that often it needs to be. This is a good tension to work with and one which adds further layers and complexities to what we do together as writers.

The weather is wild here, the tail end of hurricane Gustav is lashing the coast, ominous warnings of the winter that is just around the corner!

From Jonathan, in Abingdon

Just a quick response having returned only today from a week away: to say that I completely support the idea of exchanging tentative/incomplete/incommensurate/ unpolished pieces. I've begun a contribution in response to Ken's recent writing and have thought that I will send it as it is, sooner rather than later, however brief. So, yes, please, Bronwyn, send yours asap. Please don't do any more on it—I'm eager to read however far you've got to! Fast and short, back and forth, is good for me. And maybe these emails, to-ing and fro-ing across the world, as we are working out and developing our collaboration with each other and Deleuze, will become part of what we present at QI.

Our hesitation in getting the JKSB assemblage underway was to do not only with the lack of pre-agreed striations to order our work, but also the recognition that the opening up we were about to engage in was risky. Bronwyn asked, for example:

How risky, then, is this space we four are unfolding? I have pondered that question and I have hesitated about this beginning. I recall past wounds from other collaborations, and wonder about my own inadvertent wounding of others. One of my co-writers routinely battered my ideas as part of his taken-for-granted means of making those ideas his own. He drove me once into a kind of hysterical paralysis. For his part, he said, it hurt him that I so often rejected the pearls of his wisdom. Clearly I became the swine for him, in my blindness to his pearls.

Another, perceiving me to have much more power than I thought I had, railed against me with a storm and fury that undid me completely. How could I get to be so invested in acts of collaborative writing that they could bring me undone? I am curious about that space of investment and risk. One of the things I loved and feared about my three sons growing up was their playful, risk-taking exploration of the world, in contrast to which I saw myself as tentative and cautious. Now, in their adulthood, I think they perceive me to be the one who takes the risks...

It is not surprising, on reflection, that I have used the word love in a profligate way in describing my response to J and K's paper "two men talking." I love it because they love each other, and are so deeply engaged in the process of writing to and for and into each other. Perhaps it is that love and that engagement, along with the openness to the not-yet-known that makes collaborative writing so risky. The smooth space that Deleuze encourages us to play with is dangerous. That experiment with the unknown, that openness to difference in, and differenciation of, oneself, is what makes for life, he says. But it is necessary, at the same time, Deleuze and Guattari write, to have a toe-hold on a small plot of land that is safe and predictable:

> This is how it should be done: Lodge yourself on a stratum, experiment with the opportunities it offers, find an advantageous place on it, find potential movements of deterritorialization, possible lines of flight, experience them, produce flow conjunctions here and there, try out continuums of intensities segment by segment, have a small plot of land at all times. (Deleuze and Guattari, 2004b: 178)

Presenting the play at QI, written out of excerpts from our emails exchanged from around the world, was an amazing experience. The week before the conference we met in Chicago for a first run at putting our spoken voices into the words that we had selected from our written conversations. Before we met in Chicago we each had a very strong feeling of having come to exist in and through the JKSB assemblage in a way that was moving—not only conceptually, but also as affective, sensate, ontological beings, we had been and were moved—Deleuze would say differenciated. Our engagement with each other had opened up moments of *haecceity* or thisness, where we extended the possibility of existing outside pre-existing binaries. We met together, then, all four of us, for the first time, to read out loud what we had written, to re-imagine it as an embodied performance, to live with the presence of bodies and the vibration of sound, the moments that had arisen among us in the writing. This was, for all four of us, an emotional experience. Our voices, as we sat on the edge of a fountain in the garden near the art gallery, made the words of the play even more sensate, more embodied. The reading of the play was an *event*, a *movement*, rather than a performance of four individuals—or five if we included Deleuze.

For some weeks after QI, in May '09, we were at a loss, not knowing where to go next. Then the flow of communication became, for a while, quite extraordinary, focussing on nightmares, place, and what our writing might become. But then due to the press of work, of life events, and other writing, or perhaps to the turn that the writing itself had taken, it became erratic and uncertain. Susanne decided she needed to drop out from the JKSB assemblage for a while. Bronwyn found that neoliberal thought and practice had so taken over her university, that the only way to continue with her writing in the way she wanted to, was as an independent scholar. We all missed participating in the JKSB assemblage, but didn't seem to be able to get it going again. Early in 2010, Bronwyn visited each of Jonathan and Ken, as part of her new life as an independent scholar. She stayed with them in their homes, meeting their families and friends, discovering for herself some of the spaces that they wrote about, and the will to continue was reignited. Bronwyn offered to put together the first draft of this book, based on our collaborative writing, and to do so while she was in Bristol for two months as the Benjamin Meaker visiting professor.

The extended version of the QI play became our first plateau. The plateaus that follow on from the play take up some of its threads and extend them, and also fold out into some of its gaps and silences:

Plateau Two: Of nightmares and the ontology of place: planning the book includes the burst of writing that took place between July and October of '09 asking what this book might become, when all the while it was becoming.

Plateau Three: Sea reflections, is a series of reflections on being in place and being out of place written by Ken, Jonathan and Bronwyn.

Plateau Four: Ethics, is an extended reflection on Deleuzian ethics as they are practiced in collaborative writing as we are developing it here, written by Jonathan and Bronwyn. This plateau circles back to some of the material in Plateau 2 and extends open listening into the arena of ethics.

Plateau Five: Collaborative Writing draws some of the threads of the other plateaus together into reflections on a Deleuzian-inspired practice of collaborative writing as we have experienced it. This plateau was written by Bronwyn.

A Play on and with Deleuze and Collaborative Writing (JKSB)[1]

In which we arrange our four voices, Jonathan's, Ken's, Susanne's, and Bronwyn's, into a 4 act play. We take turns at being narrator, Jonathan for the act called The flows and the in-between, Ken for Haecceities, Bronwyn for Listening and Susanne for Writing. Gilles Deleuze appears throughout as himself. The narrator is the one who addresses the audience, explaining what we are setting out to do. All other speaking turns are drawn from our emails and are addressed to each other. The words from our email communications are re-arranged to make the ideas about and the practice of collaborative writing, with Deleuze, more accessible and more immediate.

Act 1: The Flows and the In-Between

Jonathan (as narrator): The four of us have written together since last northern hemisphere summer, exchanging writings across the ether, exploring our various understandings of how Deleuze helps us think about and engage in collaborative writing. Ken and me in the UK and Bronwyn and Sue in Australia have separate histories of collaborative writing as pairs and with others, or, as Deleuze might put it, in other "assemblages." On this plateau we work reflexively with Deleuzian concepts in order to examine our own four-way collaboration—a collaboration that we have found deeply absorbing as our words and affects form tangled lines across the globe. Out of those tangled lines we have fashioned this play in 4 acts. In keeping with Deleuze's resistance to striation and categorisation, these acts—and we—are not easily separable; they and we are felted together.

Bronwyn: Since we agreed to open up this four way conversation about Deleuze and collaborative writing, I have been trying to imagine what sort of space it is that I am entering; that is, what the relations between and among us might be, and what possibilities might open up for our/my being-writing-thinking. It is in the spirit of Deleuze that we have left the nature of the space open; it is an experiment in writing; it does not have a timeline or an order of speaking/writing laid down for it. It is smooth space, perhaps; yet I find myself looking for the striations that give me some foothold on what the possibilities are here.

Deleuze: "What mattered was not the points—[Ken, Bronwyn, Susanne, Jonathan], who functioned simply as temporary, transitory and evanescent points of subjectivation—but the collection of bifurcating, divergent and muddled lines, which constituted this [writing] as a multiplicity and which passed between the points, carrying them along without ever going from one to the other" (Deleuze and Parnet, 2002: viii).

Bronwyn: To the extent that we are persons then, we are no more than inflections on lines. Our collaboration brings lines together to see what happens when they intersect, and unravel.

Jonathan (as narrator): Collaborative writing through a Deleuzian lens seeks to cultivate the in-between, not the points, or the ends. But I want to start here with the "points," as a way of seeking in-betweens and flows. The "points" have been powerful. There have been the four of us, in our writing, four bodies walking, working, swimming, sleeping, and not sleeping. Our separateness has been present in our geography. We have written from or about different places—

Ken in Cornwall, Jonathan in Oxford and Kenya; Susanne in Sydney, in the desert and in the tropical north of Australia, and speculating about being in Nova Scotia; and Bronwyn in Sydney, too, and in Firenze in Italy and visiting preschools in Sweden. Our experiences of being in, imagining, and reading Deleuze's writings about place have accompanied us in each of these places, flowing between them in "bifurcating, divergent and muddled lines" (Deleuze and Parnet, 2002: viii).

Susanne: I have never been in snow as it falls and have never seen icebergs floating in saltwater. I hate the cold as a rule (being Australian) but it shocks me awake and there are all sorts of body blows. I wonder what other sorts of being, what other becomings might be enabled by such a big adventure to Canada. I am very interested in the possibilities entailed in being otherwise in other places.

Bronwyn: I love the feel of myself in the morning here in Firenze, when I greet others, including complete strangers, with *buongiorno*. It is warm and connecting. Yesterday I noticed eye contact and a smile. Compare it with "good morning." So cold and formal, and slightly alienating. It marks the beginning of the school day for me more than anything else, "good morning girls, sit down please"; the controlling gaze of the teacher. *Buongiorno* is rich and sensual, and somehow playful. *Grazie* is lovely too. I feel as if I have genuinely thanked someone when I use it. In Japan I used to have to add thank you in English because the Japanese words didn't carry for me the feeling of gratitude. Curious this becoming in another language, even at this simple basic level.

Later: Strawberries, fresh and sweet, doused in sugar and freshly squeezed lemon. Espresso coffee with sugar; a bottle of mineral water, under the shade of a pine tree on a hot early autumn afternoon, sitting in a café on a hillside looking over *Firenze*. A piece of heaven after the hard sweaty hours walking up the hill.

Susanne: I wanted to tell you about the desert. I ran away to an island in the desert: no electricity, phone, computer, hot water, bed, room, clean clothes. For a week I wore all my clothes to bed at the same time, wore sheepskin boots as bedsocks and a beanie on my head. I slept in a canvas bag under a fading aquarian moon and more stars than I've ever seen at once. A sea of stars above my head. Desert sand in everything.

Jonathan: I am in a hotel in Kilifi, ninety minutes' drive north of Mombasa, where I have been doing some work with scientists at a research centre in the town. The work is done and I am enjoying the day to myself before travelling home tonight.

I feel on my skin a warm westerly wind off the Indian Ocean. I often wish I were a scientist, someone who knew things. Like now, when I wish I could tell you the names of the trees and the plants around me, could name the bird that flew so gracefully across from my right and landed to perch on the fence to my left. Colours escape me too. I struggle to name shades: that second bird's brilliant blue. There: I've tried. Does that do it? Yesterday I took a boat along the creek, upstream, with a man who knew the name of every bird we saw. I liked the sounds of their names. The birds were beautiful, simply beautiful, and I wished I knew what they were. What is this longing to name? As if I could capture something in the naming; an expression of power, perhaps, a longing to conquer with words.

I am looking east along the creek towards the ocean and, beyond, to Perth, I guess, though I am not sure if the latitudes are aligned as I imagine. I think due East is probably some way north of Australia, so if I turn slightly to my right...

I have a view and setting to die for. Yet I am discomfited by thoughts of Patrick, a young man who works at the hotel. On Sunday he accompanied my colleague and me in viewing the ruins of a 14th century mosque built by the Omani traders who first colonised this part of Kenya. They traded not only in raw materials but also in people. On the twenty minute walk to the ancient mosque Patrick told me that his dream is to go to college to study computing. He is unable to do so. It would cost him over a year's wages. £400. He told me that an English couple earlier this year had promised to find the money for him: they would keep in touch, they would ask friends to help (as if they would need to, given that they had travelled to Africa on holiday), they would wire the funds direct to the college as Patrick advised. He has heard nothing from them.

Later, on the hot, dusty, return walk through the village that stands immediately outside the hotel, I was walking ahead and Patrick was with other guests. He caught me up to ask me directly if I thought that I could help. I replied that I couldn't, which he seemed to accept.

So, Patrick is with me as I write; and my discomfort is with me too. My discomfort is about being white and wealthy, of course, and about having declined to help him; but it is also about my resentment that Patrick should have laid his demand on me. Patrick is involved, uneasily, in this collaboration. So, too, are the wind, the clean white walls that I see to my right as I look up from my notebook, and the waves in the middle distance that I cannot quite hear but imagine that I can.

Ken: I have been carrying our emerging collaborative work with me, both in my body and in my shoulder bag, feeling its presence and yet skirting around it, circling the text, wanting to engage and finding it hard. Susanne has written about "being on the brink of writing, but not getting to it, or not getting it out." I have been experiencing this. Sometimes I write impulsively, compulsively, I can't stop myself; I am drawn to the writing, it draws me. Although my language here suggests a reification of the writing, it is not that. It is a deep contrast to this. In these moments of writing energy it is an embodiment, I feel suffused with my actions, the action of writing becomes me; dare I say, is me. It is in these deep iridescent crystal moments, when the lines between the outside and the inside, the refractions and the reflections become lost, that I too lose myself and in that moment of loss find discovery. Not the discovery of the excavation or the archaeology more the realisation of the epiphany.

I am addicted to this rush, this is what the writing does to me and I know this is why I return. I know, like Susanne, there are so many times when I am on that brink, wondering whether I am able to or not. Can I? What shall I write? What shall I write about?

Sometimes when I go to the sea it is like this. Now as the summer gives way to the autumn, the shivery westerly winds, the cool fresh air and the early darkness of the receding day dissuade me and tempt me away. My reticence finds 101 mundane tasks for me to do in my house and attempts to persuade me to recognise their need. Deep down something always helps me to resist. Something lurks and won't give in. It is a literacy of self that has inscribed me in these ways; has written on my body, has written my body. And, at that point of knowing, there comes a realisation that prompts a mad headlong rush of sense and value that takes me out of my house, leaving those tasks behind, a few minutes in my car and there, stumbling, clambering down the cliff to the beach and into the sea.

And then later as I shiver and tingle, alone on the beach with my towel wrapped around me, looking out at the never ending sky and inhaling the hiss of the waves, I wonder how I ever hesitated and why I ever delayed, knowing that being in these moments gives me energy and life and the vigour to carry on with whatever it is that is paining me when I allow the normality of my life to carry me along with its routines.

Jonathan (as narrator): These points, these places, these bodies, flows finding space in between. Why have we kept our own names, here, when it is the flow in-between that matters? What we hope to show, is the way the words flowed from the still points of each life, into the multiple lives, words, affect of the others. We worked toward …

Deleuze: "…not the point where one no longer says I", but the point where it is no longer of any importance whether one says I. We are no longer ourselves. Each will know his own. [In this work] [w]e have been aided, inspired, multiplied" (Deleuze and Guattari, 2004b: 3–4).

Susanne: In the desert last week I loved this quote: "Continental islands serve as a reminder that the sea is on top of the earth, taking advantage of the slightest sagging in the highest structures" (Deleuze, 2004a: 9).

Is Deleuze writing about geography? I loved the idea that the sea takes advantage of the earth. I like the cunning of the sea, its wilfulness. At a poetry festival this afternoon, one of the poets, Michael Hofmann, said that for a long time he tended not to use many verbs. He thought it was because he was nervous, shy about taking up space, being agentic. In an interview online he says "I don't trust verbs or I don't deserve verbs" (1999, np). Yet the sea here is agentic, and perhaps the earth too. The earth sags and the sea takes advantage.

The idea of the sea between us, the hemispheres, the opposition of the seasons, does surprise me. Keeps me apart. We are so far here from everywhere, especially from you. I say "we" as though Bronwyn is still here but she is far away as well now, closer to you, Ken and Jonathan. Bronwyn has been already close to each of you. In the same room, in the same time zone, the same season when the dogwoods are in flower.

Jonathan (as narrator): The earth sags, allowing the space for the sea to flow between us, the in-betweens, to become.

Bronwyn: What exist are the possible lines along which one can flow. We are constantly flowing in and out of the same/different lines. When our lines merge, we become a different line; share the journey on that line. Our writing, or music, makes the line more vivid, changes it, generates a new energy, new possible connections, new intensities. The spark leaps from one body to another. The streams flow together and make a new stream. In taking up this collaboration we open up a space of flowing together for a while, making a third stream. Or is it a fifth? The question becomes do we know the line we are flowing on/generating/taking ourselves up within/together? If we remain immune to each other, closed to each other, too much consumed by other series we are caught up in, there can be no fifth line. Most likely we will each flow for a while in the fifth stream and life will demand, daily, that we hop out of it and do the boring housework instead of swimming in the waves.

Jonathan: I find that with the four of us I often lose the sense of where I am with our writing. I feel overwhelmed by it. The flows, the streams, feel too much. In order to write I have to let go of my fantasy that I can be "on top of" it, can be "in control." I have to accept that it—they, the haecceities of our writing—is/are bigger than me, more than me (whatever "me" is).

I have not sought a link or unifying theme in this writing but there is this: that this writing does not feel separable, discrete. The writing—as Ken has often written—is me. But it is also not "me": it is all of this, all of these, it is us. It is Joe's worn-out shoes, Susanne's eyes peering "twixt beanie and scarf," red rock in the distance, Abingdon's market square, Bronwyn's writing shaking me into stillness, Ken's echoing words.

Writing with Deleuze disturbs me. Writing collaboratively requires that I let go of myself.

Bronwyn: There is no clear now, or present or past, in these reflections.

Deleuze: "It's not a question of being this or that sort of human, but of becoming inhuman, of a universal animal becoming—not seeing yourself as some dumb animal, but unravelling your body's human organization, exploring this or that zone of bodily intensity, with everyone discovering their own particular zones, and the groups, populations, species that inhabit them" (Deleuze, 1995: 11).

Jonathan: Collaborative writing through a Deleuzian lens seeks to cultivate the grass that grows between. It is concerned not with the paving slabs of our exchanged writing but with the resilient weed that forces its way through the cement that we lay between them; the unintended, perhaps unwelcome visitors that emerge through the shapes we create around and between us, as we sit back and admire the careful crafting of our landscape. Rocks, flowers, pond, trees (you might be able to tell by now that I'm not a gardener), each set out to complement, echo or contrast with the other, to form our free-flowing, wild but thoughtfully-designed garden. But, it seems, for Deleuze, it is in the spaces, the middles, the muddled flows that the unexpected opens up between us, taking us into the not-yet-known.

Deleuze: "So Félix and I decided to work together. It started off with letters. And then we began to meet from time to time to listen to what the other had to say. It was great fun. But it could be really tedious too. One of us always talked too much. Often one of us would put forward some notion, and the other just didn't see it, wouldn't be able to make anything of it until months later, in a different context. And then we read a lot, not whole books, but bits and pieces...And then we wrote a lot. Félix sees writing as a schizoid flow drawing in all sorts of things. I'm interested in the way a page of writing flies off in all directions and at the same time closes right up on itself like an egg. And in the reticences, the resonances, the lurches, and all the larvae you can find in a book. Then we really started writing together, it wasn't any problem. We took turns at rewriting things" (Deleuze, 1995: 14).

Act 2: Haecceities

Ken (as narrator): I sense in my reading of Deleuze a *creative evolution* of the self not as a process of individuation of the fixed subject or the extended corporeality of the body, rather as the becoming that is apparent in the degrees and intensities of the self that connect and multiply in relation to others, to Bronwyn, Jonathan and Susanne in this collaborative writing project. Deleuze uses the notion of haecceity to describe moments of molecular intensity when percepts, affects and concepts connect the individuating molar self in relation to a milieu of space and time.

Deleuze: "The proper name (*nom propre*) does not designate an individual: it is on the contrary when the individual opens up to the multiplicities pervading him or her; at the outcome of the most severe operation of depersonalization, that he or she acquires his or her proper name" (Deleuze and Guattari, 2004b: 42).

Ken (as narrator): So, haecceities might describe the events, the infinitives or the spaces between Jonathan, Bronwyn, Susanne and Ken as they have lived in and become through the multiple and interconnected dimensions offered in our play with Deleuze and collaborative writing. We have written across thousands of miles yet as Bronwyn says:

Bronwyn: It is as if in this writing we put our hands through the computer, and our eyes on the screen and bring to life the virtual intensity of the other; it is an intensity made possible in anticipation of the other's hands/eyes through the screen. In that sense we do not exist except in the relationality, an exchange of the virtual intensities as they are taken up in the hands and eyes and heart of another; it is this exchange, this flow, that Deleuze calls life.

Jonathan: The room where I write at home is at the front of the house, a 1930s semi-detached—does that translate?—on a somewhat drab estate. Today there are no curtains and it is dark outside. Early evening: autumn is with us. I took the curtains down earlier in the day so that we could dye them. I feel exposed. The small garden outside the window leads towards a hedge and then the pavement. I imagine that people walking past can look in and see the debris on my desk (screen, books, empty water bottle, transistor radio, pens, phone, glasses case, and post-it notes) should they wish to. A couple of times over the years I have walked out onto the pavement to check what people could see from there with the curtains open at night. Nothing. The hedge is too high and the room too far back. My worries are all my own.

Bronwyn: The painfully hesitant woman at breakfast in the hotel stayed with me all day. She had, in effect, come to life in my own body, or at least my own imagination. It occurred to me eventually that I knew her hesitation only too well. Yesterday I had been about to walk into a shop, following someone else who had just entered, but for some reason I hesitated at the threshold, not sure if I wanted to go in. A young woman rushed up behind me shouting at me in Italian, her face close to my face, her message urgent, emphatic. I stared at her in dumb wonder. She switched to English and shouted "No, no, no! Closed! Lunch! Lunch! No, no!" OK, they were closing for lunch. I had created a scene by being about to do something wrong. There were at least a dozen customers in the shop. I was appalled at her performance. But I maintained my composure and did not give way to visible anxiety or apology. I kept my cool gaze on her face-too-close-to-mine for a few brief moments and then turned, smoothly, and walked silently away. I abjected her, and in that moment she was integral to my subjectivation. I had become not-her. She was both me, and not-me, since she lived at my borders. For a second or two my affect was not unlike that of the woman this morning at breakfast, I was dazed at the disaster that I seemed to have caused, but I became not-that-woman-at-breakfast at the same time as I became not-the-woman-shouting-in-my-face.

Deleuze: "Affects aren't feelings, they're becomings that spill over beyond whoever lives through them, thereby becoming someone else" (Deleuze, 1995: 137).

Bronwyn: Last night at *La Boheme* I wept for Mimi's death and for Rodolfo's grief. All day at the back of my mind I have heard the last two words of Rodolfo's grief over and over. Mimi's name, repeated. So much grief. So much loss. The music expressed their love so perfectly, and then its loss in death. Because it was sung in a church and not on a grand stage, the singers were only feet away from the audience. I was caught up totally in the music. The flow of love and loss in the music became the same flow as my own loves and losses, no longer past, but totally present in the music that flowed through my body, one folding out into the other. The whole audience was captured in the ecstatic unfolding of love and loss, simultaneously swept up in the same affect. None of us, probably, was capable of such perfect *expression* of love or grief, but none of us was in doubt about the affect that flowed, collectively, through us and beyond us. I was amazed at the human bodies of the singers being a place where such intensity could be expressed.

Susanne: I have just come from my Tuesday night choir where we sometimes find a smooth space for a moment, an immersion, a pure connection in the sounds we make together, in how we are together. Bliss. In those moments there is an abandonment of individual subjectivity and we are becoming-other in a pure resonating space that transcends and exceeds us. Interestingly, this smooth space is only possible because of the discipline of learning the songs so thoroughly and because we have practiced practiced practiced. The smooth space in this instance requires the striated space in order to come into being.

Ken: At first I sensed my writing as a flow; words appeared to come
                easily, time drifted away, but, I guess, as tiredness began to kick
                in after another long mad busy work day, I sensed my self ago-
                nising more and more over the words, struggling with a partic-
                ular expression, gradually losing confidence with and in my
                parole. My desire to write, to be with you in the moment of writ-
                ing sustained itself, but my simple physical energies succumbed
                to the lateness of the hour. An agonising moment of haecceity,
                perhaps, captured in the multiple, flowing intensities of my tired,
                feeling body.

Jonathan: It is when I come close to understanding Deleuze that I become
                most in touch with my anxiety. The implication in haecceity that
                "subjectivity" lies beyond the physical boundaries of my body,
                that I am bound and beholden to, connected and complicit with,
                amongst others: the page onto which I'm writing on a pale
                autumn Wednesday afternoon; the wooden shelf on which my
                forearms are resting; the wonderful, inviting smell of coffee; the
                two young women baristas and their machinery behind me; the
                cold air outside that, because I am sitting near the door, hits me
                as the mother and buggy come in; the man at the table next to me
                who is always here on Wednesdays, and who seems sad each
                time, an impression I gain, perhaps mistakenly, simply by how
                he moves; the images I have of each of you as I write, my pictures
                of what you look like and where you live, and the lives you
                lead—all of these are "present" with me in these moments.
                Instead of humanistic individuals, I think about individuations
                as being constantly in flux with new assemblages being formed
                but never fully so—this is both a delight and a loss.

Bronwyn: I think this is approaching a definition of univocity; the complex
                thought of our selves as continuous with human and non-human
                others without for a minute giving up the intensity of being spe-
                cific, of inhabiting and being inhabited.

Ken (*as narrator*): As our collaborations become increasingly molecular and
                intensive the sense of distant extensive space that we four inhab-
                it seems to dissolve; as Bronwyn says of working with collective

biography: "I think the work we do...is the search for words to bring to the surface the haecceity or life of the moment, to bring images out of their shadows, and it involves sparks and flashes between one story of being and another, which gives it life in a new way, more open to the flow of the other's becoming."

Bronwyn: I have been pondering what makes for two flows to merge, or for affect to be shared, and it seems haecceity may be a key. If the moment of being is folded out into words or gestures that the other can take on, in its thisness, (assuming the other is attending) then the moment will be shared.

But does it necessarily require such attentiveness? I am occasionally fleetingly aware of my body taking on the movement of another body, perhaps when it is hunched or anxious. As the shared bodily state comes to my consciousness I straighten up, or breathe into the anxiety to let it go. I see it and I know it intimately without paying it much conscious attention. I imagine we are taking on each other's postures all the time without noticing.

When Virginia Woolf, or Proust, captures the moment of being in words, it becomes more readily available for attention—they give the moment life—not just a virtual intensity waiting to be found, but a movement to something new both for them as writers and us as readers.

Deleuze: "One's always writing to bring something to life, to free life from where it's trapped, to trace lines of flight. The language for doing that can't be a homogeneous system, it's something unstable, always heterogeneous, in which style carves differences of potential between which things can pass, come to pass, a spark can flash and break out of language itself, to make us see and think what was lying in the shadow around the words, things we were hardly aware existed" (Deleuze, 1995: 141).

Ken (as narrator): And as the virtual intensities of our collaborative writing creatively evolved, our desert seemed to become more populous, and haecceities seemed to abound. We found ourselves writing *with* difference, differenciating, letting go of familiar, repeated patterns. "[T]hings acquire fixity, that is, they acquire parts and hence boundaries through repetition" (Williams, 2003: 11). It was both disturbing and exhilarating to find ourselves intensely caught in moments of being that became our own and at the same time not recognisable through repetitions, not originating *in* us, but *with* us.

Bronwyn: What collective biography does, and our collaboration is doing, is to clear a space for speaking and listening and writing so that the haecceity of the moment is there for everyone in the full collective attention to the moment. In the everyday world there are a whole lot of things at work to make us numb to each other, stuck in a small set of striations. What Deleuze calls his vitalism, is an invitation to life, which he sees as the antithesis of being stuck. But that is not to say he is out there open at every moment. He doesn't suffer fools gladly, and he approves of still time when there is nothing to say.

Deleuze: "What a relief to have nothing to say, the right to say nothing, because only then is there a chance of framing the rare, and even rarer, thing that might be worth saying" (Deleuze, 1995: 129).

Jonathan: Williams says "When you stand, daydreaming, looking out over your favourite land—or cityscape, or staring into another's eyes or flesh, or allowing your body to become an automaton through repeated work and exercise, allowing thought and sensation to drift through you, you are closer to Deleuze's idea of the individual than when you squeeze your head in your hand, reflect and consciously toil with a problem. An individual is not a self-conscious "I," it is a location where thoughts may take place...This view of thought as independent of consciousness breaks down the difference between humans and other things. For Deleuze, the evolution of a line of animals or plants or rock formation can also be said to express ideas" (Williams, 2003: 6).

Ken: It seems to me that the reading and writing that we are now engaged in can be likened to the way that Irigaray talks of the intense sensuality and the intimacy of touch, where the "touching" and the "touched" dissolve into the moment of "touch" which, in that moment, has no separation of giving or taking. These voluptuous and agonistic collaborative actions of reading and writing talk more of what we do, not so much of who we are but more of our becoming.

Deleuze: "This intensive way of reading, in contact with what's outside the book, as a flow meeting other flows, one machine among others, as a series of experiments for each reader in the midst of events that have nothing to do with books, as tearing the book into pieces, getting it to interact with other things, absolutely anything...is reading with love" (Deleuze, 1995: 8–9).

Jonathan: There would be a problem, Deleuze would say, if the four of us were precisely persons, remaining identifiably separate. The four of us collaborating is only possible if we see ourselves not as persons but as haecceities, however "modest or microscopic." Our collaboration, our writing, is something passing through us, a current, though maybe more accurately our writing *is* us rather than passing *through* us. Even as I might think that I am writing this on my own I am writing with you.

     I wonder if I can attempt a poem about haecceity. There is anxiety here too about leaving the familiar form of prose. Poetry feels more exposing. I did think that I would leave this idea to one side for now and return to it when I felt better about myself as a writer, but I kept writing.

The endless possibilities of describing
The sound of the clock in the memory of the bereaved man
The car stuttering in the dark beyond the faded blue curtains
The uneven rhythm of pen on paper
The wearing, indeterminate discomfort of muscular tension
The imagining of others' presence
Presence
The stale warmth of the radiator
The voice over the tannoy calling "next"
The inexhaustible possibilities of this here, now,
Gone

Susanne: *Ding!* A message from an early morning Ken shoots into my inbox. His words to Bronwyn about swimming evoke the close-

ness of smooth space: "Your pool is vivid; I sense the warm
water, my arms breaking the stillness of the surface, the view. I
remember early morning swimming with my children in a pool
overlooking Lake Garda in Italy [he writes] and being so sensu-
ally immersed in the water, the view, Reuben and Phoebe's shouts
and laughter, that the troubles that were looming in my life reced-
ed into the background." Ken and Bronwyn have found these
Deleuzian haptic smooth spaces of close vision in their pools
and in their swimming. Deleuze and Guattari say of such space
that "its orientations, landmarks, linkages are in continuous vari-
ation...the desert, steppe, ice, and sea, local spaces of pure connection" (2004b: 544). I love it that the pure connection Ken and
Bronwyn find is both embodied and material—connections
exceed the human and familial but are with the water itself, the
view dipping in and out, Bronwyn lapping "on the edge of the
sea" and looking "out over the waves and dolphins and surfers
and sunrise." This seems to me the perfect evocation of this close
vision where there is no single orientation or position for looking
or being in relation: "one is never 'in front of,' anymore than
one is 'in' (one is 'on')" or like Cezanne who needs to "*no longer
see* the wheatfield, to be too close to it, to lose oneself without
landmarks in smooth space" (Deleuze and Guattari, 2004b: 544).
It is the pure wateriness, paint, colour, texture, sound, sensation,
temperature. I am strangely curious at what immersion in an
intensely cold climate would do to a person who has never known
it. What other becomings in this other place would emerge?

Bronwyn: I love this, and I love the fact that in our writing we evoke precisely this—the time of day, the wind, the heat, the excruciating
pain and pleasure of becoming in that moment.

Ken: This morning I went to work in the woods with the man I have
to describe with the cumbersome phrase "father-in-law": he is a
man who has become my friend. As his daughter and I go our
gradually separating ways I find something different in him and
I sense him also finding me anew.

It is December: eight in the morning. There is still frost
sparkling autumn's long dead leaves. The sun is highlighting the
houses away on the hill in the distance, but here in the shadow
of great towering ashes, oaks and beech, it is cold. Our breath

plumes like released serpents in the sharp crystalline moment of air and light. We look at each other. The words are unspoken but the meaning is shared; to be busy will be the only respite from this freezing inertia. We open the truck: chainsaws, axes, oilcans all give off a reeking, masculine smell. It is a relief to pick up the heavy splitting axe and to hold the shiny hickory shaft, to feel its dry bony smoothness in my hands and to move its weight to achieve balance with my body. The coughing roar of the chainsaw jerks me from the sensual calm of my reverie; I awake and become a man.

Geoff is driving the screaming blade of the saw into the great fallen boughs lying in the ferns like broken limbs in a battlefield. Great sections of log become separated from the main branch and are ready for splitting. I start to lift the ice-cold sections of wood from the sodden mess of the woodland floor. Fungi, brambles and rotten stumps all hinder my progress; they seem to be saying you are not of this space, go to your laptop, go to your writings, this is not your world. Go on.

I lift one great ring on to another, line it up so that the angle is just right, juggle the axe from one hand to the other, lift it up, back, over my head, propel it forward and then let it drop, let its weight do the work, guide it in its short, furious flight to that spot, just there and...thump, an instant rending noise and the pristine ring tumbles into two naked semi-circles. Lift one up, place it back on the sedentary ring and repeat. Crunch. A quadrant. Pick up the other semi-circle, lift the axe again, set its swing in motion and watch with pleasure as the semi-circle of beautifully grained wood gives way to the irresistible momentum of the heavy steel axe head flashing to its heart.

Now it is all about rhythm, lost thoughts, and the desire to find another ringed log, to place it on the block and to swing the axe in an effortless arc and see its amazing effects and then move on again to the next one...I am lost in this. My body glows with warm sensual pleasure; my fingers that were numb with the unforgiving icy coldness of the wet winter logs now grip the shaft of the axe with a new strength and my heart pumps with an energy that refreshes my soul.

Where is this space?

Am I in between?

Here, I am lost. I could not have predicted this. My body grows like weeds in a bomb-site; my life spins in a new direction. I find new life in the beauty of this simple activity. Here in this space, in the space that I thought was a brief in between space, a space in which something had to be done, I found for some minutes, maybe an hour, something that was me. Here was a re-membering; in the intense haecceity of this space I found something I had allowed myself to forget for a while.

Now tonight I am back in this familiar space. Now my desk lamp glows, the rest of the room is dark. Now I am tapping keys on my laptop.

My head is buzzing with words, conjunctions, flows...ideas burst and explode with every attempt to make sense. I am writing. I am visualising you Bronwyn, Susanne, Jonathan: this is the space that I have become used to inhabiting; this is where my habits have grown and invaded my sense of self.

It is good to be writing to you, for you...what is it? It is good to feel a slight aching tension in my shoulders, to feel the fresh hardness of the muscles in my arms and to live with these new scratches and the growing roughness of the skin on my hands.

Bronwyn: I remember when I lived on an abandoned cherry orchard, arriving home in the cold winter darkness with the three kids, going out in the dark with my boots on to chop the wood for the stove that heated the house and the water. Just that easeful moment of the axe falling, the cold air, the mist, the smell of eucalypt.

Deleuze: "When I said Félix and I were rather like two streams, what I meant was that individuation doesn't have to be personal. We're not at all sure we're persons: a draft, a wind, a day, a time of day, a stream, a place, a battle, an illness all have a nonpersonal individuality. They have proper names. We call them "haecceities." They combine like two streams, two rivers. They express themselves in language, carving differences in it, but language gives each its own individual life and gets things passing between them...From this viewpoint, writing with someone else becomes completely natural. It's just a question of something passing through you, a current, which alone has a proper name. Even when you think you're writing on your own, you're always doing it with someone else you can't always name" (Deleuze, 1995: 141).

Bronwyn: Elsewhere, he talks about his concepts evolving according to the task at hand, and the generation of new concepts being part of the line of flight he deems so necessary. He also strongly advocates the linking of percepts and affects to concepts, which I see as a large part of what we are doing here. We are together making a line of flight, a flow, a series of folds out of Deleuzian concepts and our percepts and affects. We are not sure where we are going but that is as Deleuze would have it—we must make our way out of the clichéd, boring, repetitive, already known and find something new. In this lies our capacity for life.

Act 3: Listening

Bronwyn (as narrator): In this act we puzzle over the apparent contradiction between the intense interest in flows and becomings, which Deleuze encourages, and the intense experience of the material specificity of individual selves. What we open up here is the idea that while there is an ego or person that is more or less abandoned in Deleuzian thought, there is at the same time an intensity between one and another that is quite singular. We perform, in this particular Act, a responsiveness to the singularity of the other that makes the other possible—not as an ego-driven "I," but as a particular responsive and provocative human assemblage. This encounter with the other, one's collaborator, who is both, at the same time, singular and plural, is an act of love. As Deleuze says of his encounters with Félix Guattari, "we understood and complemented, depersonalized and singularized—in short, loved—one another" (Deleuze, 1995: 7). Deleuze sees in this collaborative relationship the wellspring of creativity; the other mediates our capacity to express ourselves:

Deleuze: "Mediators are fundamental. Creation's all about mediators. Without them nothing happens...Whether they are real or imaginary, animate or inanimate, you have to form your mediators. It's

a series. If you are not in some series, even a completely imaginary one, you're lost. I need my mediators to express myself, and
they'd never express themselves without me: you're always
working in a group, even when you seem to be on your own"
(Deleuze, 1995: 125).

Bronwyn (as narrator): I first met Jonathan and Ken when they were presenting
"two men talking" at QI. I loved what they did there. I loved the
openness of each one to the other, the dissolving of the "you and
me binary." "Your writing comes off the page, enters me, affects"
Ken wrote, and then read out loud, with the assembled audience
almost become voyeurs overhearing the exchange. There is a
deep and risky intimacy in this exchange between two men who
trust each other, who allow us, the readers and listeners, into their
space, who tell us about becoming one another, and at the same
time evoke their separate specificities as they are made relevant
and meaningful in this flow between them. Who might I possibly be/become to them I wonder, and they to me, as I enter this
four way collaboration. None of us knows, in this Deleuzian
sense, what acts of becoming lie in store for us in the space we are
opening up.

At QI Jonathan and Ken mentioned my work several times in
their "two men talking" presentation, not knowing that I was
there also in the flesh. My flesh was unrecognised. It was a
strange moment for all three of us I think, the flesh and the words
suddenly connecting. Now, writing and performing together, it
is amazing and pleasurable to find myself captured to such an
extent.

How will it matter that we know or don't know each other?
Certainly we don't know who each of us, ourselves and one
another, might become in this new space as it opens up. Do I
know Susanne and not Jonathan and Ken? I know quite a lot of
Susanne's past becomings in the various assemblages I have
been part of with her. It's a particular knowing that comes from
the kind of listening that we have developed in collective biography—one comes to know not the person, but the singularities;
the heart beat, the intake of breath, the flash of rage, the images
inscribed in their remembering bodies, their tears, their kindness.
The kind of knowing we have sought in collective biography is
not *connaissance*, knowing the nature of the other as an object dis-

tinct from the self, but *savoir*, which involves thinking in order to
know differently, and in the process, being modified through
what one comes to know (Foucault, 2000). We listen to each
other's stories not to say I see who you are, in a phenomenological sense of you as knowable subject, but I see through the very
singularities of your stories something more about the Being in
which I and you are co-implicated. Deleuze invites us to contemplate ourselves as univocal, and at the same time continuously
differentiating, becoming different in each moment, each move
ment.

Susanne: A week later, another Saturday. Bronwyn is now in Florence
              flooding words and I am here in a city inundated by rain but I feel
              like I am out of words. In the text I started writing last week I
              pulled out more quotes from Deleuze and the desert island essay
              and then something must have interrupted. Finding this daisy
              chain of quotes again, I thought I would delete them. How could
              they still be relevant when such a chunk of time has passed?
              How many people—a hundred, more—have I had to interact
              with in a single week at work? Does each interaction overwrite
              the lingering ones that are not yet complete (or in this case, not
              yet begun). But instead I keep them here. I'll work my way up to
              them, write my way in, and muse around them.   My inclination
              is to tell you where I am right now but, as you all know, too much
              of it is tedious, and too much of it is work, there is too much of
              a tendency to document the tedium...

                There seems to be a yearning with me always now for more:
              more time, more time to write, time to think into spaces where
              writing might come. Not papers but poems.

                Deleuze loves language too, that much I can tell. That wins me
              over. It's always won me over. Bronwyn too, as your beautiful
              Florentine writing shows, loves language and the greatest per-
              mission that she gave me—an imperative really—was to write
              beautifully, and so I tried to.

                Today I was at a poetry festival in the city—I want to go again
              tomorrow—though the long days do me in. I have to write a lec-
              ture about poetry for Monday but not the way I'd like to write
              about it, about loving words and the way they fill the mouth and
              spill over at the edges of the heart. The tremor of the old man in
              the yellow cardigan this afternoon, launching his chapbook,

"Scenes from a marriage," knocking over furniture, trembling as he read, stopping in the middle of his own poem—at the wrong time—to get his breath back as he tells how the breath went out of his wife, and their first child 25 days old and dead and was always with them.

Deleuze: "In the act of writing there's an attempt to make life something more than personal, to free life from what imprisons it. The artist or philosopher often has slender, frail health, a weak constitution, a shaky hold on things: look at Spinoza, Nietzsche, Lawrence. Yet it's not death that breaks them, but seeing, experiencing, thinking too much life...There's a profound link between signs, events, life, and vitalism: the power of nonorganic life that can be found in a line that's drawn, a line of writing, a line of music. It's organisms that die, not life. Any work of art points a way through for life, finds a way through the cracks" (Deleuze, 1995: 143).

Susanne: From the desert I have a notebook of half-written pieces. In my two weeks holiday soon, I have promised myself I will write nothing but poems, or movements towards poems. I will have to undo some parts of the person I have become so that I might do this.

I feel too much of the time that I am on the brink of writing, but not getting to it, or not getting it out. I can be prolific—as Bronwyn will attest—but to me none of it seems to come fast enough, nor, more importantly, do they come in the right order. Is this a sort of sagging? I think I lost interest in myself last week, in what I was writing, when I started citing properly and using phrases like "our colleagues." Perhaps there was a sense of sagging, of myself sagging into academic rhetoric. I want language to be buoyant, perhaps like the sea, playful enough to take advantage.

Ken: I have been immersing myself in the lovely writing that Bronwyn and Susanne have sent in the past few days. I am full of wanting to respond and am trying to work myself into a space where I can do that.

It is really good to have the experience of this work together:

I am finding my way in this experience and feel strong about being and being enveloped in what we are doing and will continue to do.

Jonathan: I have the four of us in mind. Our physicalities feel present and significant: we are in four different places in the world—Bronwyn in Italy, Susanne in Australia, Ken at home in Millbrook and me here. We are far apart but I am connecting with you inside, or wanting to, wanting to find you, find us, in this writing. I am interested in this newly-forming configuration and where it might take us. It is risky, yet full of promise, as Bronwyn suggests—"a venture into the not-yet-known." I have pictures of you in my head: a Ken that I feel familiar with and imagine that I can see (though, with Deleuze in mind, I understand that he is becoming-Ken and not the same Ken as I spoke to before I left), a Bronwyn whom I remember sitting to my left at the back of that small classroom in Urbana-Champaign eighteen months ago, and a Susanne, whose session with Bronwyn at QI in 2006 I attended. I sat towards the back in a room full of people and only caught a glimpse of you.

I am back home now, and have both Bronwyn's and Susanne's beautiful writings to fold and unfold myself into and into my writing.

Ken: This last week or so has been so exciting, receiving writing from you all, Bronwyn, Susanne and Jonathan, from all over the world! The locations are all, in their different ways, so important and the evocation of place in your writings has been so powerful and such a joy to read. I want to try to write a little about that and about the people that inhabit these spaces and, perhaps, a little tentatively, about us and our writing together.

Bronwyn the lovely images of your days in Florence washed over me. The heat, the pastel shades, the warm sensuality of your words marked me with their simple intimacy and intoxicated me with their potency. I have sat here at my desk this screen glowing. I have done this so many times before; it is so much a part of my life but today, perhaps, more than any other as I read those words I became aware of the physicality of the writing and its contexts. All of us here in our spaces, connected to the other as bodies in our relative "realities."

As I read your words I was also so aware of Jonathan there in Kenya absorbing and reflecting on life in that vivid and vibrant world in thoughtful and sensitive ways. So Jonathan when your writing from Africa arrived I felt washed again, feeling the sense of flowing in benign currents, happy to allow myself to go with the ebb and flow, enjoying the imagery of the birds, your views and the poignancy of your encounter with Patrick. Always being with you in the multiplicity of our space, knowing you in different ways through the rich engagement with your words. In the last few days as our writings have crossed continents I have become aware of the urgency created by the spaces we inhabit. Sensing you Susanne in your fur lined boots and beanie hat, huddled in the harshness of an unforgiving desert climate but sensing also the way in which that experience began to take you to the "yearning with me always now for more: more time, more time to write, time to think into spaces where writing might come. Not papers but poems." Yes, I know that: "Not papers but poems"!

I have lived in the world of sense and value that all your lovely writings have given me: from the warm and rich sensuality of Florence, from the harshness of the Australian desert to the vibrant, exotic colours of Kenya. Outside the window here in Cornwall the weather is unkind: cold sleeting rain pours from the sky and lashes against my window; I lean my body up and forward, looking to the west, eager to catch a glimpse of blue sky or to begin to feel the slow growing warmth of sunlight on my face. Through these writings, so rich in their evocation of place, I gain a real sense of you, each of you, in different ways; in this writing, in my reading of your words I sense you, my knowings of you are becomings.

I have been feeling my way into the way we have written about the spaces we inhabit; in this flurry of writing we have exchanged experiences of our recent life in Australia, Florence and Kenya with such richness, warmth and tenderness. It is the people we meet and make connections with that are so important; the way that Bronwyn and Jonathan both vividly conveyed the warm generosity of spirit and welcome in their experiences of "buon giorno" and "jambo" touched my heart. The delicacy of your heartfelt portrayal of Patrick has stayed with me Jonathan, and Susanne your sharing of the "tremor of the old man in the yellow cardigan" at the poetry reading brought tears to my eyes;

your words took me there, with you, with him. I have been thinking about us in relation to all this, trying to feel myself into our
writing together, unsure where to tread, saying something and
not sure that I have said what I wanted to say in the way that I
wanted to say it. Unsure and perhaps a little unsafe: feeling a little vulnerable perhaps?

So these stories we have told of others are so important, they
seem to tell us about our worlds of connection, through our collaborations, correspondences, communications and, surely,
friendships. As we tentatively begin to open up these boxes and
allow our stories to fly we are not only sharing our experiences
of others with one another we are also storying our selves and
perhaps in so doing creating lines of flight that allow the opportunities for further collaborative work together to emerge.

Bronwyn: There are moments in the lines of writing that Ken and Jonathan
and Susanne have sent where the flow of affect enables me to
know them, to feel our hearts flowing in the same stream. Ken's
immediate worry about the situation at work, and his earlier
anxiety when we took so long to respond to his writing,
Jonathan's desire to know how to name the colour and his delight
in the beauty of the bird. (I find myself wanting to imagine exactly the blue that he saw, but not knowing the names of the birds
or the colours either, and yet also wanting to know them. I settle
on a deep royal blue close to black.) Sue's desire to write poetry,
yet overwhelmed by the expectations and pressures of work.
Jonathan reading Deleuze, and writing, while on holiday. (How
often I am reprimanded for working when I should be "relaxing,"
it is a relief to be "in flow" with someone else who knows that
desire.) Jonathan's concern about Ken. These moments live in me
as I read and write and explore Firenze.

Today I visited an orphanage, *Speddale degli Innocenti*. Built in
1419, it was a place where women with unwanted babies could
pass them, anonymously, through a rotating door, never seeing
what lay behind—never seeing them again. What became of
them? No doubt the boys became castrati, and perhaps the girls
too learned to sing and to play instruments. In a painting repre-
senting the Madonna of the orphans all the children had one
eye a bit skewed, as if it was impossible for them to look clearly
ahead with both eyes. Their faces were happy enough but their
eyes suggested a deep and terrible, inwardly turned sadness. (It
was in anticipation of such sadness, my own and my unborn

child's, that led me to marry instead of putting him up for adoption—with devastating consequences.)

I am thinking of the man in the yellow cardigan, and Ken being so moved at the image Sue drew of him, and then me finding Ken's image of tears in his eyes moving. I contemplate the yellowness of the cardigan in my mind's eye and realise it is an improbable buttercup yellow. It was probably more like mustard, but I have bright yellow in mind, and an image of a man painted by Andrew Wyeth sitting alone on the side of the hill with his jacket blowing in the wind. The image of the man is thus in a virtual series. Williams points out that "signs are not a matter of correct interpretation or reading, they are a matter of a necessary experimentation with what the sign triggers in the individual" (Williams, 2003: 53).

But why an improbably buttercup yellow? Perhaps because that is the most intense yellow I can think of and the man has taken on a particular intensity within the JKSB series. I am altered by the yellow cardigan and its presence in the series of our exchanges: In Williams' words: "Through its repetitions, through the way it creates the new by selecting what to repeat, any individual is not only the expression of virtual intensities and ideas but also an event that alters them" (Williams, 2003: 20–1).

Deleuze: "[Nietzsche] gives you a perverse taste...for saying simple things in your own way, in affects, intensities, experiences, experiments. It's a strange business, speaking for yourself, in your own name, because it doesn't at all come with seeing yourself as an ego or a person or a subject. Individuals find a real name for themselves, rather, only through the harshest exercise in depersonalization, by opening themselves up to the multiplicities everywhere within them, to the intensities running through them. A name as the direct awareness of such intensive multiplicity is the opposite of the depersonalization effected by the history of philosophy; it's depersonalization through love rather than subjection. What one says comes from the depths of one's ignorance, the depths of one's own underdevelopment. One becomes a set of liberated singularities, words, names, fingernails, things, animals, little events: quite the reverse of a celebrity" (Deleuze, 1995: 6–7).

Bronwyn: I see the kind of personal writing we are doing as a striving after this depersonalisation, finding the lines of multiplicity, recognising one's own deep ignorance, mapping the psyche precisely in an attempt to go beyond the essentialising and limiting discourses that confine us as this particular (possibly boring and mundane) person. When I say I'm not interested in myself as an individual, but as a resource for thinking, it is this kind of thing I am after.

Deleuze: "Take Foucault himself: you weren't aware of him as a person exactly. Even in trivial situations, say when he came into a room, it was more like a changed atmosphere, a sort of event, an electric or magnetic field or something. That didn't in the least rule out warmth or make you feel uncomfortable, but it wasn't like a person. It was a set of intensities. It sometimes annoyed him to be like that, or to have that effect. But at the same time all his work fed upon it. The visible is for him shimmerings, scintillations, flashes, lighting effects" (Deleuze, 1995: 115).

Bronwyn: I had the image just now, now I'm back in Australia, as I wondered how we four were, how the JKSB series was going, of "voluptuous collaboration," which is how one might characterise the J–K collaboration, Or Sue's collaboration with her colleague in the U.S. Or Deleuze and Guattari. (The children in one of the preschools I visited in Sweden, who had been studying light, described the two spots of light (red and green I think) which became white when they overlapped, as two lights kissing. A kind of voluptuous combination of two different intensities to create a third. Like Deleuze's third stream.)

Ken: Bronwyn, what a lovely image that the children from Sweden provided of two lights kissing! The individual intensities of red and green (kiss) producing a combined one of white as they overlapped; a third intensity emerging from the original two (kissing). I sense this image as I consider how we might write and read each other's words. Until I received your last piece of writing Bronwyn I hadn't thought about us all engaging in a voluptuous collaboration or, as you also suggested, that this is what Jonathan and I had done.

I really feel able to work from what you have suggested here. I have become so accustomed to living with and working from

a Deleuzian kind of logic of sense, so to anticipate, say, the voluptuous swell of exchanged writing, is both evocative and enticing.
Sinking into a voluptuous repose reminds me of the fold, of what
Deleuze called the "art of living," of that place where we can *be*
for awhile before lifting our selves up, before moving on, taking
a new line of flight perhaps.

Jonathan: I always carry with me printed copies of writing to respond to.
Ours—I see the sheets of paper as "our" writing though it is
only yours that I literally carry (mine are inside me, I guess)—
ours have been with me every day, inside my notebook, as I've
travelled to work. I have read your writings in snippets, turning
and returning to them. I note how I have missed passages, not
registered them. I like this finding something new, though it disturbs me too. I've forgotten the order in which you sent them but
it seems not to matter. The writings are flows and intensities
that, appropriately, I can't fully hold onto. I am transported to
Firenze one moment, then to dreams, then to the intricate detail
of Deleuze, then to the remote house in the tropical north of
Australia where I know Susanne has been but must by now have
returned from. In reading again some of what you have each
written, I feel as if I am in a dream, its scenes and pictures passing in front of me.

Some such scenes surprise me and I am suddenly alert. Is it
for the first time that I have read Bronwyn's bracketed sharing of
her decision to marry? I am in the autumn sunshine of the market
square as I read this now, and I pause to look up. I must pause. I am
shocked that I missed this, missed the poignancy and the pain that
I read into it.

On Monday, Ken and I ran the first of our sessions at Bristol
on performative and collaborative writing. Travelling together on
the bus from the train station we talked about this group, us, and
our writing. We wanted to offer it to that afternoon's group, to
communicate its richness, to say "Bronwyn has written this about
Deleuze, Susanne has written this about writing, Ken this,
Jonathan that," but as we were saying this we knew that we
wouldn't; we knew that our collective writing was only ours, for
now at least. I was reminded of the risks we take when we write,
the trust we place in each other, "how delicate our connection,"
as Sue writes of her earlier collaboration.[2]

Yet, even though we did not use this group's words, my experience of our writing was "folded" into the time we spent on Monday afternoon. I knew something of the experience of thinking with, living with, writing with, Deleuze, beyond the between-the-twos of Ken and me. Beginning to write as the four of us has given me that.

Deleuze: "Félix and I, and many others like us, don't feel we're persons exactly. Our individuality is rather that of events, which isn't making any grand claim, given that haecceities can be modest and microscopic. I've tried in all my books to discover the nature of events; it's a philosophical concept, the only one capable of ousting the verb "to be" and attributes. From this viewpoint, writing with someone else becomes completely natural. It's just a question of something passing through you, a current, which alone has a proper name. Even when you think you're writing on your own, you're always doing it with someone else you can't always name" (Deleuze, 1995: 141).

Jonathan: Writing with Deleuze disturbs me. Writing collaboratively requires that I let go of myself.

Bronwyn (as narrator): And so we circle back to our beginning, to the voluptuous idea of writing collaboratively as a disturbing act of love. An act in which we become more vividly real to ourselves and to each other, than we would otherwise be, in which the intensities and flows create series that run through us, and that open up the possibility of thinking, within this new assemblage, in ways we might never have been able to think before. We are not in that act of becoming specific persons identifiable through our egos, but specific beings in our multiple interconnected expressions of our mutual humanity. We listen intently to each other, we allow each other to run through us, we know each other as intimately as we know (and don't know) ourselves. We gift each other with an attentiveness that is life-giving, life-shifting.

Act 4: Writing

Susanne (as narrator): We return to writing in this final act on this plateau, although we never left it. All we have done has been about and through writing and the Deleuzian tricks and traces that we've

played with and that have played with us. "We began in summer," Jonathan once said, but the world was topsy turvy already
in any geographic, hemispheric, seasonal references. We began in
August, which in Australia can be the cruellest month, a long
dragging month of frosts that seem never to end—at least in the
mountains where I am. Bronwyn is near the coast where the sea
breeze of the bay tempers everything. Writing, more than anything, for us has been about writing in place, writing place, writing ourselves in place both materially, where our flesh is in time
and space and relationality as we write, and imaginatively—
yearning across vast distances but with our bodies in place tethered to the "small plot of...land" (Deleuze and Guattari, 2004b:
178) from which each of us write, each time we write.

As Ken says, no matter what we were doing, all the time we
were writing.

Susanne (as narrator): Another principle emergent in our writing was that other
sorts of language, logics other than the rational, were in operation. Increasingly we took up an aesthetic, even at times poetic,
mode of writing. We took our lead from Deleuze who says that
philosophy, the arts and sciences offer different modalities or
ways of being in the world. Did we abandon philosophy for the
pleasures of writing? We don't think so.

Ken: Writing becomes a crucially important means of nurturing aesthetic and ethical sensitivities. In this "logic of sense" (Deleuze,
2004c) the continual creation of concepts becomes a volatile and
transgressive mode of practice. The dynamics of this multiply
when we consider and then apply ourselves to the connections
that we have with others: we do not write in a vacuum. To use the
language of Foucault we are "situated," we inhabit "sites"; we
live, breathe and interact with others. When we write we have
others in body or mind; even our most private writing makes
some connections with others in the past or the present even if the
others of the future are kept waiting at the door.

Susanne (as narrator): Desire is integral in the assemblage of us writing. In a
filmed interview with Clare Parnet intended to be shown after his
death, Deleuze emphasises again that desire always flows into or

from an assemblage or an aggregate, desire is constructed via an assemblage (Stivale, 2000). In this text we are an assemblage, a desiring machine, a writing machine—made up of we four and of more—rays of sun, coffee shops, tables, midnight writings, sons and daughters, lovers, longings—inscribed in the small contour that our project is making on the infinite plane of writing.

Bronwyn: So what are we here, the four of us? Angels in flight, at play with words? ungendered at last, since we are neither two men, nor two women talking? working both from the heart, and without organs at the same time? What concepts can we use to grasp the intensities and the fluidity of being and becoming without ditching the heart, the gut, the brain, the skin, the genitalia? And who do I mean by *we* in this question about want? We four of course, at least to begin with. I am feeling my way into your words and bringing them to life in my present mo(ve)ments, in my becoming different in response to others (including non-human others) with whom I find myself engaged—not just you, Ken and Jonathan and Susanne, though primarily you—but also the people who come into my life here in Firenze, that I greet in the morning in a new language, the people I encounter in paintings, that I encounter in the books I am reading, my past co-authors, the food I eat, the colours and shape of the land I am in.

Deleuze: "Language is a painting or a piece of music, but a music of words, a painting with words, a silence in words" (1998: 113).

Jonathan: I am at home writing, with you, the wind, the view, the memories, Patrick. And with Deleuze. I have both Bronwyn's and Susanne's beautiful writings to fold and unfold myself into and into my writing.

Writing in Kilifi, sitting by the hotel pool, taking in the setting, I had gone as far as I could. I needed to get up, walk around, do something different. My attention span when I write is short. I make myself write a page, double spaced, and then take a break. It makes me a slow writer and not prolific (which Ken and Susanne have both referred to being and Bronwyn surely is). I share Susanne's sense of much of the time "being on the brink of writing, but not getting to it, or not getting it out." I am the last to begin writing amongst this new group of four and I feel under pressure. I know that it is a pressure of my own making. I am typing earlier than I would normally in an effort to get something to you quicker. And I expect that it will not be so long as your pieces. I can be competitive but competitiveness feels out of place here. I have no need to be. But I feel there is a lot to live up to. Will this be ok? Will I be good enough?

Susanne (as narrator): Friendship for Deleuze was important in his writing and philosophy. His friendship with Guattari could be understood as "discreet" in terms both of "discretion" and of "discontinuity"— not a friendship that "creates 'fusion,' intimacy, confidences or causes each to 'lean on the other's shoulder'" but "friendship without rivalry, without effusion" (Maggiori, cited in Stivale, 1998: 6), a productive creative smooth space. In our writing, friendships emerged tentatively, degrees of intimacy became established, smooth spaces opened—though not easily or always, or without danger.

Deleuze: "One's always writing to bring something to life, to free life from where it's trapped, to trace lines of flight" (Deleuze, 1995: 141).

Bronwyn: I think Susanne's passion for poetic writing contributes strongly to the first part of *délire*, and that its converse must also be there in the hard analytic work. Perhaps this is one of the ways in which we have worked well as a team, bringing these two sides of the coin together. Not that we either of us should be seen to be working on just one side of this "logic of sense."

Susanne (as narrator): Art and philosophy, philosophy and art. Percepts and concepts chase each other through our texts.

Deleuze: "And then thinking's a capacity, a capacity to set forces in play, once one understands that the play of forces doesn't just come down to violence but is to do with acting upon actions, with acts, like 'inciting, inducing, preventing, facilitating or obstructing, extending or restricting, making more or less likely...' That's thought as strategy. Finally, in the last books, there's the discovery of thought as a 'process of subjectification': it's stupid to see this as a return to the subject; it's to do with establishing ways of existing or, as Nietzsche put it, inventing new possibilities of life" (Deleuze, 1995: 95).

Bronwyn: It is interesting to think of us as collaborators engaging in thinking, in thought as a process of subjectivation. By introducing multiple voices and very different life histories into the mix we facilitate the process, perhaps, of seeing our own thinking in process, generating traps, backwaters, or ways out. Thought itself becomes more visible and particular thoughts become less pressing or necessary; within a collaboration one might let go where alone one would hold on, or take something for granted that collectively becomes visible (though it is also true that collaboration can be the reverse of this where your co-author holds you back). In being surprised by another's entrapment or movement, one can become more conscious of one's own.

Deleuze: "It's nothing but *délire* and madness...We need both to cross the line, and make it endurable, workable, thinkable [*Susanne*: writeable]. To find in it as far as possible, and as long as possible, an art of living. How can we protect ourselves, survive, while still confronting this line, [*Susanne*: while writing this line]? Here a frequent theme of Foucault's comes in: we have to manage to fold the line and establish an endurable zone in which to install ourselves, confront things, take hold, breathe—in short, think. Bending the line so we manage to live upon it [*Susanne*: write along it], with it [*Susanne*: into it]: a matter of life and death" (Deleuze, 1995: 111).

Bronwyn: Don't you love that? Out there on the edge and at the same time somewhere safe through the mechanism of the fold. Life and death. Take flight with something new, but keep yourself safe. For me, maybe the wild unmanageable line is turned into a safe space in the act of writing (which is similar to Ken saying on email today that he would write his way through a bad situation). The manageable space of writing is safe, but it also maybe, if we are lucky, contains the seeds of something new. But the bit about

breathing is also important—there is a safety in holding the body
in particular ways, and I forget to breathe far too often.

Deleuze: "There's a profound link between signs, events, life, and vitalism:
the power of nonorganic life that can be found in a line that's
drawn, a line of writing, a line of music. It's organisms that die,
not life. Any work of art points a way through for life, finds a way
through the cracks" (Deleuze, 1995: 143).

Susanne (as narrator): Deleuze writes about writing for illiterates, for animals,
writing as change, as passing from one state to another, writing
as becoming:

Deleuze: "...writing as a rat traces a line, or as it twists its tail, as a bird
sends out a sound, as a cat moves or else sleeps heavily. Animal-
becoming, on condition that the animal, rat, horse, bird or cat,
itself becomes something else, bloc, line, sound, colour of sand—
an abstract line. For everything which changes passes along that
line: assemblage" (Deleuze and Parnet, 2002: 56).

Susanne: I began an earlier version of these writing notes with some words
I loved from Patricia Ticineto Clough:

"She told me that when she read what they said she had written, she could not imagine that it was she who had written it. She
could not grasp its meaning. She worried if, in fact, someone else
had written it. Or was it written in code? And if so, code for
what or for whom? When I asked her if these were the right
questions, she told me she did not know for sure. And after a
short hesitation, she told me that she wondered if she should not
write what had been written. Again" (Clough, 2008: 140).

Deleuze: "The writer twists language, makes it vibrate, seizes hold of it,
and rends it in order to wrest the percept from perceptions, the
affect from affections, the sensation from opinion" (1994: 176).

Ken: Ideas burst and explode with every attempt to make sense. I am
writing. I am visualising you Bronwyn, Susanne, Jonathan: this

is the space that I have become used to inhabiting; this is where my habits have grown and invaded my sense of self.

Bronwyn: Ken's words draw me into the present moment, the moment of our writing, the moment when I don't feel sad or alone, but connected and intrigued and pleased to be alive. I often turn to my writing and thinking to avoid the sadness, or the ongoing anguish of human relations, and this writing is not like that at all.

I have been pondering lately what we choose to tell each other and what we leave out. Sometimes we hint at huge life dramas, and tell very little. Sometimes we tell of one of those life-making moments that is both nothing and everything. Sometimes big things happen and they don't make their way in.

Deleuze: "To write is certainly not to impose a form (of expression) on the matter of lived experience. [It]...moves in the direction of the ill-formed or the incomplete...Writing is a question of becoming, always incomplete, always in the midst of being formed, and goes beyond the matter of any livable or lived experience. It is a process that is a passage of Life that traverses both the livable and the lived. Writing is inseparable from becoming: in writing, one becomes-woman, becomes-animal or vegetable, becomes-molecule..." (1998: 1).

Susanne: ...becomes us and undoes us.

Notes

1. An abbreviated form of this play appeared as: Wyatt, J., Gale, K., Gannon, S. and Davies, B. (2010) Deleuzian Thought and Collaborative Writing: A Play in Four Acts. *Qualitative Inquiry 16*(9) 1-13.

2. Ken and Jonathan did not discuss JKSB with their other writing group (e.g. Gale et al. 2008, 2009), nor Gale et al. with JKSB. The sense of the privacy of the writing, referred to here, was strong despite in each case an intention to publish.

Plateau Two

Of Nightmares and the Ontology of Place

Planning the Book (JKSB)

This Plateau is a series of emails about nightmares and the ontology of place. These emails were ostensibly about planning the book, something we had trouble envisaging. It includes the burst of writing that took place between July and October of '09, asking what this book might become, when all the while it was becoming.

From Bronwyn 12–7–09 (6 weeks after QI)
Dear JKS,
I am curious about where we are headed. Jonathan has offered to sketch out a possible book for us to work on. I'm wondering in what way it will grow from our play and the work so far. Will its focus still be Deleuze and collaborative writing, or will that be one thread in a larger whole? Maybe we need to bounce some ideas around to inspire Jonathan???...

From Jonathan 16–7–09
Dear BSK,
Sending you the email earlier in the week seems to have freed me to be able to think and last night our writing formed part of my dreams. I awoke this morning with thoughts that I wish to offer. For me, the richness of our writing last year was in its flows and lines of flight. We did not know where we were going, made no particular plan, only gave the loosest (though sharpest, too) of briefs, to explore Deleuze and collaborative writing. And

look where it took us?! There's so much that we left out of our presentation too. So I wonder: how would it be if we simply gave ourselves the same mandate from here? We could loop back to where we have already been (as Bronwyn suggests); we will each be in differing and changing geographical, intellectual, emotional and life spaces from which we can write; we can allow each other's writing to lead us; and we can keep in mind always that we are continuing to write with our fifth group member, Deleuze himself.

Would this work? I guess it will feel different that we do not have the QI gig as a goal; but would, instead, a book work as our goal? We could agree to write for, say, the next year then review what we have and where we have been and see how we might shape our writing into a book. I guess it's different from how many books get written, where there's a proposal first, a plan, an order, and then people write. But, when I've been thinking about that, that seems to feel constraining. The risk is that we might write and then find that no one wants to publish a book along whatever lines we have gone. But I bet we'll have a good time in the process.

What do you think? (I know that Ken is in Barcelona as I write so will not be able to respond for a while.)

Thinking of you,

JONATHAN

From Bronwyn 17–7–09

Dear JSK

I am sitting in the winter sun on the back verandah of my friends' holiday house in Beechworth in Victoria. The sun is intensely hot; it is one of those beautiful blue sky, still days after frost. From the verandah I can see the garden that slopes down to the creek, and on the other side of the creek a granite rock face that soars up the side of the mountain. In the immediate foreground is the duck pond that Johanna and I built last year. Johanna had figured that there was a natural spring and that the granite might be in the shape of a pond. We dug out wheelbarrow loads of dirt for one long sweaty day until finally our pond began to emerge. The wild ducks have now colonized it, and other birds come there too. Kookaburras, on hot hot days dive into it to cool off, and at the moment galahs are also hanging about. All sorts of wild life come to this garden—wallabies, koalas (well, at least one) and an incredible array of birds. This morning when we went for a walk along the gorge we saw a group of gang gang cockatoos—who have grey and black feathers and a bright red crest. They were eating something in the huge tree they were in, which sounded like nuts being cracked open with their strong beaks, yet it was a gentle sound like heavy rain drops falling.

This area is vulnerable to bushfires, so there is no guarantee it stays here forever. The house is on the edge of one of those small historic towns that has been beautifully restored so it has a very evocative early Australian settlement feel to it. It is so peaceful to be here in this beautiful space and with such dear friends. Coq au vin is about to be served for lunch out on the verandah.

The bushfires have given us here in Australia a jolt into the new era we live in, of uncertain futures. The world I was born into in the 40s seemed utterly stable. Things were built to last. The cycle of seasons was predictable. One could learn where the dangers were and avoid them. Now we exist in a time when the Deleuzian flows that take us to the not-yet-known may be incredibly dangerous. My kids grew up with the horror image of nuclear war. Now climate change necessarily shifts the way one looks at the landscape, as something even more transient than we could ever have imagined—at least than those of us not born in war zones—could ever have imagined. So—I'm sitting here pondering the book we will write. I imagine a series of plateaus. One plateau might be place, and relation to place. It seems all 4 of us are very much moved by (held by) the spaces we find ourselves in. Another might be listening, since that is not a topic I am not at all ready to let go from my thinking. How will each of our separate lives and intellectual pursuits/questions/passions weave themselves together in the space of our writing? thanks J for getting us started.
Love to you all

B

From Ken 23–7–09

My friends
Tonight, I have been sitting by the beach, quietly on my own, living my life with the sun going down.

I raced down the motorway from working in Bristol today with Jonathan, Jane and Nell, knowing where I had to be for the last hour of daylight, that first hour of darkness and the wonder moments in between.

In that lovely in between time I drank some beer, was deafened by the sea and lived in the madness of loneliness.

I am so glad that we will write more/that we are writing more.
I love it when Susanne says: "writing about Deleuze does my head in" and then follows it with "I love what we did and I think we should do more of and with it"!! That seems to be it! Every time we do it, it is an adventure: he does our heads in, but we still try him out and suddenly we all come alive in the space that writing with him, to and from each other, seems to open up. I have just been reading his first book on Cinema; I thought I would try something new! Hey Susanne it did my head in! I took him to Barcelona with me and on Sunday afternoon, sitting in the mad baking intensity of Gaudi's Park Guell, I

felt his movement-image in Gaudi's voluptuous, oozing architectural shapes and designs. I let my head go, my senses soar and got it in that intensive moment of heat, passion and perfume!

So yes Jonathan "we will each be in differing and changing geographical, intellectual, emotional and life spaces from which we can write; we can allow each other's writing to lead us; and we can keep in mind always that we are continuing to write with our fifth group member, Deleuze himself." That's great! That's a real capture! I am glad that he does my head in too because it allows all the other mad disconnecting and re-connecting parts of my body to whiff his scent and chase him around and come up with something new each time.

I have spent five wonderful days in Barcelona, with a friend and I couldn't believe the effect/affect being there/being with was having on me all the time. Now I re-read your message Bronwyn I am acutely aware that I am "very much moved by (held by) the spaces (I) find myself." I loved the intensity of getting lost, sometimes at night in scary ways, coming out into squares where crazy tattooed jugglers were spinning fire and where mad poets were shouting at walls. I couldn't believe the beauty of wandering in the cool quiet of a deserted lane, with narrow buildings towering above us and then slipping quietly, without plan or directed conversation, into a tiny bar to sip cafe solo and brimming glasses of Fundador and to find a whole new world opening up. Bronwyn, at first I shivered when I read again your words: "Now we exist in a time when the Deleuzian flows that take us to the not-yet-known may be incredibly dangerous." but I find as I grow older now, the world of the "not-yet-known" is a very precious place to be. It is a place that when I look back on it I struggle with but I am encouraging myself to be in more and more. As I try to unwrap myself from the burdens and still living tendrils of a body with organs that won't let go of me, I know in my feelings and my values, in my heart and in my soul that there are other lives out there/in here.

So, right now, I am not sure how "each of our separate lives and intellectual pursuits/questions/passions (will) weave themselves together in the space of our writing" but I want to write to that and with you all to see where it might take us. It feels to me that the spaces that we have opened up so far have been rich and exciting, vibrant and new and I just would love to have more of that.

KEN

From Bronwyn 23–7-09

Dear JKS

I have put our emails into a Word file—since I think it was me who began the bad habit of responding in the body of the email, which then makes it an unwieldy text to work with later. I'm suggesting we go back to attachments, though admittedly there is something very immediate and compelling about the email format.

I am this week reading JK's book, and loving it. I feel as if I have a whole life-time of tellings to write to you and that something of about the size of a book is about to pour out of me. But first to the prologue that I've written...But before that—a connection in the JKSB2 series. Last night I woke in a sweat at midnight. I was exhausted from only three hours the night before and needed to sleep. But the nightmare I was having was so dreadful I forced myself to wakefulness and got up for a few hours to let the vividness of the nightmare pass. I was in a huge dark multi-storied house, and there were luminous worms and small snakes wriggling and writhing on the floor, and a murderer who was, one by one, killing the children. Two were already dead in far corners of the house, and the only way to save the third was to wake and stay awake. When I woke, I thought—so he's back, and he still wants to kill us...[cut][1]. Now, I am really aware of the delicate path we (JKSB) tread when we choose what to write. What does it mean if we tell each other things that can never go out into the public world, because it is too complex and threatening for people we love? Is it better not to write it in the first place, or can we confidently say it's ok because we'll edit it out later?

When we began this JKSB series, I thought it was risky. I guess it still is sometimes, as J reminded us when he thought to withdraw. But still, even despite that, it seems to be a space in which the unsayable and unsaid can come out onto the page safely, because of the quality of listening that greets the words on the page. The quality of listening and the absence of clichés. The kind of collective reflection that opens up new lines of flight—where the monster can provoke us into new embodiments, new flows, if we let it—or maybe not, if he is too hard. He can lie there on the page, and the words flow over and past him.

From Jonathan 29–7-09

Dear all,

I've written this brief piece in response to our recent writing. I worry that it is something of nothing but I wanted to get something to you sooner rather than later so here goes. We hear from Bronwyn that life is hectic, Susanne. Hope it slows soon.

Love to you all,

JONATHAN

Disorientation and Stillness

I have been clumsy this morning. I tried to pour water for myself with one hand whilst holding coffee in the other and, unable to separate the plastic glasses, I managed only to knock a few over and scatter them onto the floor. I replaced them on the shelf, having finally decided that I should perhaps put down my now spilt coffee, but noticed as I left that the vigilant barista who had been observing my struggles duly put the dropped glasses in the bin, presumably for reasons of hygiene. Barely a few minutes later, a moment ago, sitting at my table, I swept over my coffee whilst reaching for my bag on the floor beside me.

I've been wondering why this clumsiness has been manifest, and I think that it is because my equanimity is disturbed. I have read our recent writing, which ends with Bronwyn's dream. I am playing, over and over, the line "so he's back, and he still wants to kill us," and I have, ever so slightly, collapsed.

The beginning of the dream, as Bronwyn describes it, gives us a sense of the unfolding violence and of Bronwyn's beginning fight against whatever it is that is causing such unnamed, invisible horror. She then wakes and she—and we—understand, with a start, exactly what its origin is. He is back. On hearing, on re-reading, that sentence I am unable to hold myself together. I start knocking things over, balance and coordination gone. I wonder, in shock, if this is my own violence unconsciously being displayed. Am I—are we all—somehow implicated? Or perhaps it is my fear. He is back, whoever the "he" is that I see.

Bronwyn tells us more about the he who is back, her efforts over the years to deal with him, the effects of those efforts on those she loves, and her resolution to face the task now facing her.

I said in my immediate email response to Bronwyn's writing that I was stilled. I am stilled again now. First stillness, then disorientation, then stillness again. Both at once. The stillness is prompted by Bronwyn's noting of the fragility of this writing, the "delicate path" we tread as we write together.

I am taken to Ken's picture of Barcelona at night. First, the disorientation in:

> the intensity of getting lost, sometimes at night in scary ways, coming out into squares where crazy tattooed jugglers were spinning fire and where mad poets were shouting at walls.

And then to the stillness:

> wandering the cool quiet of a deserted lane, with narrow buildings towering above us and then slipping quietly, without plan or directed conversation, into a tiny bar to sip café solo and brimming glasses of Fundador and to find a whole new world opening up.

I slip between one and the other, from the nightmarish juggler to the quiet awe of steepling buildings and back.

Bronwyn answers her own questions about risk—"what does it mean if we tell each other things that can never go out into the public world?"—by affirming, tentatively perhaps, that ours is a space in which the unsayable can indeed be safely written. We can work at transforming our monsters through the writing, using them to provoke us into new flows, flows that cover or sweep past, that create new movements and new shapes.

I feel humbled by our responsibility to find embodied ways to hold, disrupt, be in, become in, this space. In my familiar psychodynamic ways of thinking, I think about the therapeutic space as one that needs to be sufficiently "contained"—safe, held, boundaried—for play, creativity and healing to take place. I remain at ease with this but I find that the space that writing can offer is also a space of disruption, of troubling, of disturbance. Ours, maybe, is sufficiently contained for us to be able to entertain disruption. Maybe that is how transformation can take place.

Or perhaps I am being unrealistically optimistic. I don't wish to be suggesting, simplistically, that writing can make the nightmare disappear. I keep on hearing "He's back and he still wants to kill us," and it does not become easier. That it is written, however, may be something.

JONATHAN

From Ken 2–8-09

I have just read Jonathan's most recent piece and wanted to say how connected that I feel to you all through his writing. I have had to rush here to write this fragment to you. I have Reuben and Phoebe with me and we are engaged in all the lovely busy/ness of our life together but I wanted to say that I re/cognise so much in Jonathan's words and that I want to be with you in this writing. I want to be in these thoughts of disorientation and stillness and to feel and respond to the recurrent wash of Bronwyn's dream. So I am here, full of the moment, and looking for a time to write!
love to you all

KEN

From Susanne 2–8-09

Hi all, Sunday night thoughts about the cracks of time attached, love Sue
Dear JKB(S at least in the textual sense?),
My word for the day is "inchoate."
Main Entry: in·cho·ate
Etymology: Latin *inchoatus*, past participle of *inchoare* to start work on, perhaps from *in-* + *cohum* part of a yoke to which the beam of a plow is fitted being only partly in existence or operation : **INCIPIENT**; *especially* : imperfectly formed or formulated : **FORMLESS, INCOHERENT** <misty, *inchoate* suspicions that all is not well with the nation—J. M. Perry>
It seems somehow apt.
Excuse my silence but I knew that your messages needed time, attention, thought, clarity, care, responsiveness, listening in the ways that B's message

unfurled so beautifully. I have been somewhat inchoate: unable to start work on, somewhat "misty." The word popped out fortuitously in a spell-check of a paper I sent to B earlier. "Incorporate" became "inchoate" to the little guy inside my computer who checks the words because I left out letters, in my haste. Letters, words, paragraphs, sometimes when I'm as busy as this I lose days (Monday is suddenly Wednesday) or whole weeks—thinking for example that it is already next Sunday night (although I would be at the theatre then as I already have the ticket). I certainly lose thoughts and I lose the right moment to respond in the right way.

In a way this is an existential clumsiness not entirely unlike J's disorientation, with my clumsy veering about amongst thoughts and affective responses. I hope you don't mind if I speak to another corner of my experience. If we could colour our messages, I know that is a "cool" response into a space that is "hot." Perhaps this is something that I do sometimes despite myself, because of myself. J asks what writing can do to a nightmare. What writing can do, takes me through a different crack in time. The most extraordinary moment early in my return to university was when I read the remarkable chapter "Women's subjectivity and feminist stories" in Ellis and Flaherty's (1992) *Investigating subjectivity: Research on lived experience.* It was of course by B, as she was at that time, and was in part about some aspects of the events that resurface in memories often and in dreams from time to time and of which she has sometimes spoken (Davies, 1992) I think it was extraordinary because I remember so sharply where I was when I read it (and I have read so many books in so many places since then). I lay on the sofa with the little ikat fishes in my cool downstairs up there, when I lived in a hot and lovely place. My feet remember exactly where they would make contact with the bamboo of the sofa, what I could see from there, the blues and whites and greens in my peripheral vision. Needless to say, it blew my mind. It was completely remarkable to me that the interrogation of lived experience of this sort could be academically legitimate. It was this chapter, and the one by Laurel Richardson on "Louisa May" in the same volume— these two more than anything else I had ever read in academia, or perhaps even have since then– that drew me in. They fired me up and allowed me too to start analytical and discursive work on my own life. Or should I say, to move from the textual to the personal, that it was B's generosity that did that: firstly in allowing me to enrol in a subject out of sequence which should not have been on offer that year at all, secondly in allowing me to invent my own assignment, which was a direct response to both those papers (and eventually became the first paper I ever published in QI) and thirdly, in providing such a generous response—a long letter back to me which evidenced a deeply personal engagement with what I had struggled with textually and theoretically, and what I struggled with (and continue to) as a fatally straight feminist woman. Although these may seem procedural or marginal when they were afforded to a student

she did not know who lived in another city, these small kindnesses were profound in their effects. My experience was as though this near stranger had
known me, had listened to me in my singularity and particularity with a quite
remarkable care.

I go back to our "play" on listening but cannot find quite what I want to
loop back to there, but I do find this: "In the act of writing there's an attempt
to make life something more than personal, to free life from what imprisons
it..." (Deleuze, 1995: 143). I think there is more (for you) to do on listening B but
it's interesting that a search for listening brings me back to writing. In the
vignette that I sketched of the woman on the sofa reading and how that began
an engagement that led to this moment, that "listening" was materialised in
writing. I remember B's tiny handwriting across about four pages of good
paper. Quite a different response to an assessment grid or rubric such as those
we are compelled to use now, in some misplaced bureaucratic gesture towards
equity. A grid doesn't listen. A grid doesn't care. A grid can't tremble, can't find
the point of resonance between your story and mine, between "us" in this dis-
persed assemblage. A grid can't spill coffee.

Deleuze says the act of writing can make life free, as it moves beyond the
personal. I know the nightmare does not go away, nor the story that is always
part of B and the others whose story that is. Perhaps there will be a time when
the novel that she wants to write about it can be written. Or the right conditions
for writing something for someone will emerge around this story. How to
move (further) beyond the personal in the writing seems to be the crux and the
key.

I see the therapist in J's writing: kind and comforting. Hopeful. Inevitable.
But a good way to be I think. And part of the arsenal we all enlist, some with
more need than others, against nightmares. And in the face of which nightmares
become weak, diffuse and through which they dissipate.

Other questions that arise: Is there an unsayable in this space? I think so.
I think an unsayable might be when assumptions are made that might be hurt-
ful to another. Is this a safe place? Not entirely. Not intrinsically. But I think we
are all mindful and engaged in an endeavour to keep it so. Last year that
meant an occasional turning away from something I couldn't engage in argument about, or felt defeated by. So I think silence or delay is ok, there are
many reasons for it, not all of them the most obvious ones. Sometimes we might
not reply in any authorised or regular order.

Looking back over the writing again—I have a picture of Ken as a little
dog, racing madly around a park sniffing out the scent of Deleuze, just vanished
from the scene/ sight/ seen. I don't know what dogs there are in Cornwall but
a mad little scruffy mutt (my favourite sort of dog actually) comes to mind. Or
wandering (mutt-like) in the laneways, amongst mad poets and fire-twirlers.
That works for me more than Fundador (perhaps because I don't know it and

am sadly reminded that I have not yet been to Barthelona). I have no such material space to offer you—it's just been work space and office space and car space between one and the other for weeks. (Though there is still a faint blurr of Connemarra green on the horizon of my mind).

[Also, by the way, the book...I want to do both—have the play expanded into book chapters (please a longish timeline) and follow whatever red threads emerge for us].

I started with a long quote I gathered that seemed to frame all I wanted to say but as I've written more and more in front of it I have pushed this text all the way to the end. I've made no explicit use of it although reading this was where I started, and what started me writing. I love the "bloc of childhood" here, the other blocks of being that our memories (our nightmares, our dreams) "cracked" us in to:

[With Deleuze's idea of the crack of time]...it is unclear whether one is in the past or the present, resulting in a haunting in time, of time, a folding of time... For Deleuze, the imaginary should not be reduced to the individual subject's unconscious. The imaginary does not just belong to the subject or even to the subject's body. The imaginary is part of a machinic assemblage, which may include the subject, but does not do so necessarily. As Pearson argues, Deleuze treats memory "not as regressive but as creative, a shift from its function as a psychological faculty of recollection" (Pearson, 1999: 196). Rather memory is conceived "as the membrane that allows for correspondence between "sheets of past and layers of reality," making insides and outsides communicate" with the potential to swerve to the future (Pearson, 1999: 196). Memory intervenes and intensifies, opening up new paths.

Memory becomes a block, a "block of becoming" that allows lines of flight, of inventiveness, through transversal communication, that is to communication without any fidelity to genus or species, or a hierarchy of forms. There is a creation that involves deterritorialization, which however is not regressive; it does not presume loss or a lack in the being in the subject, as the psychoanalytic treatment of trauma does. Even the thought of childhood memories must be rethought. As Deleuze (and Guattari) put it: "We write not with childhood memories but through the blocs of childhood that are the becoming child of the present" (1994: 168). This writing block of childhood calls forth experimental writing that constitutes not merely an experiment with a given form, such as experimenting with the ethnographic form. It is rather an invention that strives to capture a shift in thought happening to the writer and which the writer is inviting. Each writer is thrown backward and

forward to find the self that is turned into parts, turned around parts
of a new assemblage, an autobiographical-techno-ontological writing block. (Clough, 2007: 14)

PS I just fell through a crack in time when Sunday nights used to be Disneyland
on TV and cosying up with toasted cheese sandwiches in our pyjamas. Damn,
why didn't we recognise that it wouldn't get much better than that when we
were there. Now I've got to go and make faux-cassoulet and read ethics appli-
cations.

From Ken
"Go ask Alice/I think she'll know" (Slick, 1966)
Space and time. Susanne's writing reminds me of Alice tumbling through those
dimensions to find herself in the strangest of worlds. I sense myself on that sofa
in that "hot and lovely place" and can visualise worlds similar to that of
"Disneyland on TV and cosying up with toasted cheese sandwiches in our pyjamas." The re-constitutive force of such re-memberings is powerful and deeply
affective; as I read Susanne's words I sense nostalgia and a certain yearning for
these times and spaces taking me into a world of meaning making which
begins to find itself as I am driven to write to you all here and now (space and
time).

I have been stumbling through my life. I have not been spilling coffee,
although Jonathan's experiences of stillness and disorientation as he conveyed
them to us makes deep resonant vibrations in my chest, like the heaving drone
of a didgeridoo or the back rhythm of a trance dance track. In my stumblings
I have found myself lurching into worlds of affect and percept that have de-sta-
bilised the worlds of reason and concept that I use to fabricate the sanity of my
life. As I write now, remembering our past writing about and with delirium, I
feel so thrown off the rails of meaning that I have attempted to lay as a means
of ordering and shaping my life as a father, a lover, a teacher, a writer...It is as
if I have become undone.

I wonder how much this stumbling resembles the Deleuzian stuttering in
the language that we have already talked about in our past writing. When
Jonathan describes himself as being "clumsy" as he knocks over the coffee and
then on reading Bronwyn's account of her nightmare of having "collapsed," I
wonder how much this talks of worlds of corporeality, of forces and our figu-
rative representation of these things. "I start knocking things over, balance and
coordination gone." I imagine our bodies without organs being clumsy and
stumbling as they engage with the disorientations that come about as we live
in the aesthetics and irrationality of worlds of intuition and sensation. It is the
unified regulated organisation of the body with organs that Deleuze challenges, not the organs themselves, so it is conceivable that as we open up, as

we become undone and live in these vibrant new worlds of transgression, experimentation, transmutation and flux we will stumble and from time to time, space to space, fall. In *Francis Bacon: The Logic of Sensation* Deleuze says: "(A)t one and the same time I *become* in the sensation and something *happens* in the sensation, one through the other, one in the other." (2004b: 35). So our stumblings, our stuttering, our clumsiness are perhaps suggestive of what Deleuze calls "allotropic variations" (2004b: 45) where we are experiencing the quality of existing in more than one form. Jonathan reads Bronwyn's account of her dream and collapses: this is not surprising if we see it in terms of a Deleuzian intensive reality. Jonathan has not simply read about the dream with his eyes and formed a concept, gained a meaning or owned an understanding; the account of the dream works on him in the world of reeling senses, shattered emotions and pulsing values: who wouldn't collapse under such an onslaught!

Susanne's writing casts me into child space and time. I think of Deleuze when he says:

> In the case of the child, gestural, mimetic, ludic, and other semiotic systems regain their freedom and extricate themselves from the "tracing," that is from the dominant competence of the teacher's language—a microscopic event upsets the local balance of power. (Deleuze and Guattari, 2004b: 16)

It is almost as if the spilling of the coffee is OK! It is as if the gesture, the intonation, the unintended word, the tease, prompts and becomes a new world of thought, of affect or of interpretation. It is troubling. I too am drawn to Bronwyn's dream and I shudder. I sense Jonathan's "clumsiness" and briefly reside in an empathic knowing. I ease into Susanne's sofa and, for a moment, relax. As I write these words I sense a noticing, which connects me to Bronwyn's lovely words that have helped me to understand listening in such powerful ways. It is as if this noticing becomes through our writing, it is as if these "microscopic event(s)" might have passed by without our words to represent them and yet, in these differentiated and multiplicitous ways we sense each other; our ontologies, if only briefly, intertwine. It feels to me that our writing here, to, from, within and between our bodies without organs is taking place on a "plane of immanence":

> (I)t is a plane upon which everything is laid out, and which is like the intersection of all forms, the machine of all functions; its dimensions, however, increase with those of the multiplicities of individualities it cuts across. It is a fixed plane, upon which things are distinguished from one another only by speed and slowness...The

> one is said with a single meaning of the multiple. Being expresses
> in a single meaning all that differs. What we are talking about is not
> the unity of substance but the infinity of the modifications that are
> part of one another on this unique plane of life. (Deleuze and
> Guattari, 2004b: 280)

As I interrogate my own writing "blocks" and as I begin to shuffle through the world of my own stumblings I am finding myself, I am setting out "modifications," finding myself erasing some of the tracings that I have allowed to form a picture of my albeit confused subjectivity. I keep returning to these microscopic events and in noticing them and in paying attention to them I find myself destabilising the molar world that my sketching and drafting attempts to create. I imagine Bacon in his studio, pulling out a canvas from a stack in the hall and making changes to the forms that had lived on them in a previous world of sensation, always working, making changes, living with the body, ever presently aware of their always changing morphologies.

So, drawn like a moth to a flame, I relentlessly burn my wings as I allow this affective performativity to continuously become me, searching for new meanings, understanding new conjunctions and transmutations and troubling over an unexpected frown. The siren call of this world of concept, affect and percept tempts me with its erotic mystery; I love giving in to the temptation to be curious, to trouble and to sniff out something new. (I think your image of the scruffy dog, racing around, nose down, searching out the source of an enticing fragrance has helped me here Sue: Ken-becoming-animal!). It is so exciting to live with the taste of the exotic, to briefly capture the elusive attention of someone who attracts you, to sense the energy of a new and exciting transgression. But these molar striations are ever present, they creep up on you and insidiously order and frame, they are like the grids of the policy technologies, to which Susanne refers in her most recent piece, that govern so much of the creativity and imagination that we try to bring in to our teaching and learning practices. Being aware with Deleuze that "(t)here is no ideal speaker-listener, any more than there is a homogenous linguistic community" and that "(t)here is no mother tongue, only a power takeover by a dominant language within a political multiplicity" (Deleuze and Guattari, 2004b: 7). I am drawn into critical, affective and interpretive noticings of these "microscopic events." On this plane of immanence I find myself, ever sketching, ever drawing, ever allowing new lines to reach out and to intersect, all the time intensely relishing the multiplicity that this brings, inhabiting worlds in which I am always feeling undone.

Sometimes feeling undone is OK.

It is OK as I write here with you now. I feel that the spaces which we have grown through our work allows me to express these concerns and to live with certain vulnerabilities.

It is OK as I work as a teacher, with my students, using different practices to inquire into worlds of epistemology and methodology, aesthetics and ethical sensitivity, always exploring something new and imploring a continual questioning of the ever newly old.

It is OK as I sit with my friends in the pub or at dinner together, as our conversations swing us from convention to intimacy and back again, where our joustings and meanderings take on agonistic and voluptuous forms in the growing and alluring mistiness of the night.

It is OK when I read Bronwyn's chilling observation that "Now we exist in a time when the Deleuzian flows that take us to the not-yet-known may be incredibly dangerous." Yes, with Bronwyn, I sense the dangers. I see the effects of majoritarian neo-liberalism on our worlds but I also sense with Soyini Madison (2010) that our minoritarian acts of pedagogy and inquiry can be "acts of activism," that our agency as teachers and researchers can, perhaps, have influence and facilitate change.

Sometimes it is not:

It is not OK when I sit alone with the pure shimmering intimacy of crystalline moments of person(al) reflection surrounding me, when I awake in the morning and my heart aches and I don't know why, when my sweating skin loses its impermeability and my insides and outsides dissolve in an opaque, intangible mass, when my ontology allows me to live in my body without organs, when the this-ness of the moment gives me life with no need for intellect that is separate from feeling, value or sense. It is being very present in these moments, when my anxiety takes over me, when the rush is too much and it is too late to do anything about it. It is as if the seemingly temporal and spatial loss of my extensivity takes me into a world of intensivity where the reflections and the refractions are blinding, where I lose my sight, where the glare of multiple and incessant microscopic events takes my vision away. I know they are there, I squint and peer into their burning incandescence but I cannot see. They are like a million fireflies burning my eyes, so that when I look away the searing molten scars that remain flash in an array of luminous greens, purples and yellows. My impaired vision becomes distracted, the hallucinations are vivid but I know the trip has to end and that when it does my memories of those intensive microcosms will remain without explanation, with confusion, in their complexity, without my knowing, nurturing my fragility and disabling my ability to break out of the careering encirclings of my insanity.

Then, I am not so sure.

From Bronwyn 11–8-09

Dear JKS

There are so many things I have to say into our JKSB space. Where to begin? I want to make some reflections on the JK book that I've just read in order to write the foreword for it. I want to respond to the recent writing following on from my nightmare. And I want to tell you about Badiou and make some suggestions for our writing. Maybe I'll start with the nightmare.

Nightmare reflections.

I was so afraid that that particular nightmare would recur and haunt me. Partly I suppose as I had for so long equated "retirement" with my marriage—a no-space, a place of personal non-existence, a loneliness and aloneness in the world that came close to undoing me completely toward the end of my 5 year long marriage. Of course "retirement" (at least the way I am doing it) is nothing like that. It is, if anything, more engaged with the world than "work" was. And central to that of course, is being a member of the JKSB series. I could tell it to you and know it would be heard. That is a rare and extraordinary thing. Despite the fact that it was so hard to hear, as Jonathan's response showed so clearly, I could trust that you would hear it. So the very fact of telling it to you inside the space that we have created (and go on creating) meant that the thing I was afraid of was no longer there.

Responses to the JK book (Gale and Wyatt, 2009).

I have written the *Foreword* for a general audience and because of its genre and purpose did not circle in on some of the particularities that I wanted to talk about. I want to write to you now about the beatings in the name of spirituality that Jonathan experienced as a boy, and the imagined therapy session between the two of you. I'll start with the second of these.

The moment when Jonathan says that he can't go on, is for me intensely interesting and I don't know that JK did it justice. For me, the words that J utters in his mind's eye as he thinks about how to respond or not respond needed more attention from the 2 of you. Ken from the beginning is talking intensely, completely present in the haecceity of the moment, of what he takes to be the two of you there in the moment. But J is not fully there in the moment. He is overwhelmed, he asks calculating questions of himself—should he speak or resist speaking, for example. It is, in my reading of it, a betrayal of the between-the-two that comes about through the ritualized discursive practices of therapy, but is an unbearable rupture or break in the flow in-between JK. J cannot bear to go on, but Ken does not want to let go of his moment of this-ness, which he wants to tell Jonathan about. He demands Jonathan listen to him. He does not understand that for Jonathan the "therapy" causes an unbearable break in the flow-in-between, and he goes on.

When I saw this performed at QI (Gale and Wyatt, 2008a) I was shocked by J's withdrawal, and I was *with* Ken's refusal of that withdrawal. In coming to it again on the pages of the book, I read it completely differently as I lived inside the unbearable break that the reflections-as-usual created for J, and I wanted K to understand them, to look at them, to see and appreciate J's response. I kept thinking of course the therapy session can't go on. These words make it impossible. It must stop. And somehow all the post-reflections never *got* that.

As to the beatings (which I wryly thought of as early training in S andM) I was fascinated and appalled at the brutality and J's (un)willing submission, and the parental neglect (that all parents are guilty of) that allows a young person to go out into the world and be brutally treated. How could they/I be so stupid? Somehow in the post discussion of these beatings, the brutality seemed to become unproblematically linked to spirituality, and the spirituality the thing that needed to be affirmed. I couldn't go along with that link. Desire for spirituality, even a problematic linking in the mind of the young J, yes, perhaps, but not now, in retrospect to be seen as a straightforward linking. The sexual pleasure and perversion of the one doing the beating can't be removed from the equation. This troubled me a lot in the reading of it. Too much affirmation and not enough serious challenging to the abuse.

These are of course only my (mis?)readings.

Badiou.

I came across Badiou's *Ethics* (2002) only by chance. When I sat down in the sun over breakfast to read it, I experienced an intense joy. It was as if I had been waiting to find this book. So many things I had been struggling to say or think he had articulated so clearly. I thought this is why I resigned my job, so I could be free to discover this book and sit here in the sun reading these words...

When I began to read Badiou on ethics, all troubled thoughts of an emotional return to the troubled space of my marriage and its dark fears evaporated. I was transported into a space of high creative energy and delight. Each day I spent a couple of hours reading him, usually over breakfast in the morning winter sun. One cup of coffee and porridge somehow lasts perfectly over the space of that reading. Then I turn to the multiple writing tasks or admin tasks that have to be dealt with, with the lightness of being, the excitement staying with me for the rest of the day.

Needless to say, I would love it if we could think about Badiou in relation to our writing. The first part of the book *Ethics* gives a scathing deconstruction of ethics as it is currently known and practiced today. I would be really interested in doing some focussed thought on ethics-as-it-is-practiced/imposed on us, and what it does to our writing, thinking, being, practice...

From Jonathan Montjaux. 15–8–09

I am thinking about the JKSB series, seated on the first floor balcony as our warm first day dies. I am in Montjaux ("Jove's Mountain"), twenty kilometres north-north-west of Millau in southern France. We are staying, after a gap of three years, at David's, Tessa's father's, house. I feel an urgency to write this, to "capture" for you the beauty of this first evening here after two long days at the wheel.

The village wraps itself around Jove's south-eastern torso, and I look from here back towards Millau, though we can't see the town as it's hidden behind the hill that stretches in front of me in the middle distance, Jove's cat, perhaps, asleep on his knee. Millau is somewhere behind Jove's cat, beyond whom I can see the tips of six of the seven pylons that support the magnificent Norman Foster designed Millau Viaduct. Their single white lights (at dark they turn red), flash in unison. Beyond them are two further lines of mountains on the horizon.

It's the silence I must tell you about, though this silence is frequently punctuated by sound; but there is no traffic and few people, just the birds calling occasionally and Clever Sheep's bell jangling as she eats. René, the farmer, whose house is a few doors down, an hour ago brought Clever Sheep and her dozen or so companions from where they graze during the day, the field to my left, along the narrow road underneath the balcony to the meadow to my right, where they munch away during the evening and presumably sleep.

Clever Sheep is the only sheep who has bell status. This is because she is clever. Of all of them she is the one on whom René can rely to know where she is going on their familiar diurnal journeys, so she tends to take up the front to lead them (more or less) to the correct field while René follows at the back. She is not flawless, however, and René often has to call and run ahead to gather them back from the wrong turn she has taken. As they passed the house earlier, two Silly Sheep dropped their shoulders and feinted to come into our open front door. They would have succeeded had René not been alert. But then, maybe they're not Silly Sheep at all but, rather, Feisty Sheep; and Clever Sheep is just Goody-Two-Shoes Sheep.

The silence. A faint sound of a stream running. The hum of an outsize bug. (Fly? Wasp? Hornet? I have no idea. It was stripey.) A woodpigeon.

There are trees. I am running out of words and devoid of knowledge of the natural world, as you may remember from my attempts to describe birdlife in Kenya a year ago. There are trees that sweep from the end of the rough gardens, which drop away from the other side of the road, in an arc around to the near side of Jove's cat. Some trees I now know to be deciduous and a few, in clusters, evergreen. Tessa, who sits opposite me on this narrow, wrought-iron, vertiginous balcony, is still chuckling because as I was thinking how I might write about this scene to you, I asked her, "Are all those trees"—pointing yonder—"carnivorous?" I knew it wasn't quite right when I said it but couldn't think how. She is relishing Joe's arrival with two friends tomorrow evening so that she can tell him.

The sun is down and the cicada orchestra is tuning up. It is so good to be here again. David and Tessa's mother, Dorothy, bought the house as a shell twenty years ago and gradually turned it into this simple, comfortable home. It was being used as a barn by René's family at the time so Feisty Sheep would have had the run of it. The last time we were here, in 2006, was the (northern hemisphere) summer after Dorothy died that January.

Darkness approaches. In the far distance to the south (to my right) the yellow lights of Roquefort-sur-Soulzon are now visible, sitting below a rectangular, limestone mountain. The mountains come in unusual shapes here. I will research the geological history sometime (and then promptly forget it). Many of them have flat tops, as if someone has bitten off their peaks. It was probably Jove. Or his cat.

I have reluctantly come inside to write. Tessa has gone to bed early and, as the darkness fell, I laid down my pen and stayed as long as the mosquitoes allowed. The stars were slowly emerging, the brightest low in the sky above the Millau viaduct, which now has red rather than the white lights it had at dusk. I meant to tell you that Roquefort is home to a deliciously strong, creamy blue sheep-milk cheese.

My final thoughts before the mosquitoes won came because I could still just make out Goody Two-Shoes (GTS) Sheep's bell above the now ebullient cicadas. I started to think how, in JKSB, we might each be cast as members of René's flock. I imagined I might be GTS Sheep (I see myself sometimes as too sensible and wish I could be dangerous) and Ken and Susanne the two Feisty Sheep (full of life and curiosity, and slightly mad). Bronwyn, I haven't yet observed the sheep you might be. I'm waiting to see them tomorrow morning as they head towards Daytime Field and hope to spot one sheep courageously trot next to René to persuade him that he could free himself, and the sheep, if he were to choose to, from his oppressive, patriarchal shepherding; and then she might run ahead alongside GTS, put a front leg around her and gently and warmly encourage her to wander into smoother space.

Enough anthropomorphising. I risk caricaturing and striating each of us.

17 August

This evening, before the sun has gone down and the cicadas have begun, the main sound is of cows chewing. The evening before last they were at the other end of the field in front of me, out of earshot.

The sheep went past fifteen minutes ago. Next door, the boys (Joe and his friends, brothers Gareth and Rhys) are quiet. It has been hot today and we have recently returned from river swimming, some wandering in Millau, and stocking up with provisions.

I have begun to read Badiou.

I have never seen so many butterflies. They congregate on the lavender bush towards the end of David's garden, which is just the other side of the road below. The lavender's scent is strong here.

I have been thinking about Bronwyn's comments on JK's book, and how we did not pick up on the violence. I've been thinking about this alongside the violence that Bronwyn herself writes of. Until Bronwyn pointed out that we took up the theme of spirituality and ignored the violence, I had not registered that this had been the case. Ken and I have never talked about that episode, either, as far as I remember. I'm not going to go near it tonight, not now that the lights of Roquefort are beginning to flicker, GTS' bell is ringing intermittently, and Tessa is lying on cushions, eyes closed, opposite me.

18 August

Tessa has written a poem about Dorothy: seeing Dorothy's handwritten labels on jars of jam, Dorothy's dresses that still hang in the wardrobe and as Tessa herself misses her footing on the uneven steps and floors, she hears Dorothy do the same. But, slowly, the house is losing her. There are fewer reminders than three years ago.

I notice how I am writing about Tessa more than I usually do. She is rarely near me when I write at home. Today, the boys are canoeing and I am having late morning coffee at a specialist tea house, Affini-thé (do you see what they did there?), on the narrow Rue Peyrollerie in the old quarter of Millau. There is no *délire* here, not the vibrancy of Barcelona that Ken describes, but gentle and meandering suits me today. Tessa has left her too-hot Rooibosch tea to root around the tiny shops. Many sell *produits de cuir*, leather being the town's speciality.

21 August

I realise after a few nights that the cicadas strike up their rich sound in two layers. There's the string section, which make the dominant, somewhat frantic, sound; and there are the horns, who sound mellow and are more occasional, as if it is really too warm to make that much effort.

I dreamt last night that I had returned to work early from my holiday because our car had broken down. Colleagues expressed sympathy. One, who was a colleague in my dream, I recognise as a young, Spanish man I have recently finished seeing for counselling. In my dream he offered to lend me his car and I cried and cried at his generosity. Tessa last night also dreamt that I cried.

22 August

It's the long vowel sounds I love. I am sitting at a café in St Affrique, this Saturday morning. Walking through the market, I heard the long "oo" of *caillou*, the "ay" of *travaille*, lengthened by the "y" of the double els, and the opening and closing of the mouth in *noir*. I speak the language when I need to but, this trip, I'm finding my accent causing amusement to waitresses and waiters, shop assistants and the like. This is slightly humiliating but entertaining for others.

St. Eulalie. Don't you just love its sound? Eu-la-lie. Feel how it drapes around the tongue.

I've not brought Deleuze with me and I am not yet getting on well with Badiou. I feel Deleuze's absence and found relief when I found these words in some notes I made a long while ago about the basic unit of writing being the *assemblage:* the idea with the word with the concept, etc. We have maybe used this quote before but it struck me just now, with JKSB in mind:

> The utterance is the product of an assemblage—which is always collective, which brings into play within us and outside us populations, multiplicities, territories, becomings, affects, events. The proper name does not designate a subject, but something which happens, at least between two terms which are not subjects, but agents, elements. (Deleuze and Parnet, 2002: 38)

I am feeling our assemblage powerfully here. I am an agent and an element of JKSB (and other assemblages, not least those who are currently wandering St Affrique). I feel us, JKSB, as "something which happens."

26 August (our penultimate evening)
René whistles to his sheep as he walks along the road towards them. They respond as he approaches with an immediate chorus of bleating, though "bleating" is not right. These sheep don't bleat. Their call is a yearning, a sound heavy with lack. Or so it seems to me and my projections.

The storms of yesterday have passed. The evening is again warm and the sky to the east a light pink above a thin strip of grey cloud. The wind picks up. The cicadas, the lights of the bridge (white still), the first orange tremblings of the distant Roquefort, the four young people (Holly arrived a few days ago) content next door after a day's canoeing and a good meal, Tessa reading on cushions again at the opposite end of the balcony—and I am in love with this moment.

9–09-09

Hello all,

I realise that I haven't yet commented directly on Bronwyn's thoughts about our writing in her most recent piece.

And I say—yes, yes, yes. I'm not sufficiently involved yet in Badiou and would value some to-ing and fro-ing amongst us about him, some steers here, some questions there but I very much like the direction this takes us in.

I hope all is well.

JONATHAN

From Bronwyn

Dear JKS

How I loved receiving J's writing from France. I found myself transported into that space, not just as a space that existed without any of us in it, but as a co-extensive space, with the relations between the mountain and the house and the people there with Jonathan, that were simultaneously woven through the words on the page to include us too in that space, in knowing it with you. I printed and took it with me to the coffee shop to read many times. I worried that I didn't reply straight away, and wondered why no-one else did. We have all been slow to respond lately with life taking us off in different directions.

Today I have worked all day on my Pierre Rivière paper. It is one I have been working on, on and off, for a couple of years. Because I am doing something with Badiou in it, I thought it might be good to get it into good enough shape to send you before taking off to Scandinavia on Monday. So you can see what it is Badiou is opening up for me in my thinking (in response to J's email below saying it would be good to get some thoughts rolling on Badiou to see if we want to do anything with him in the JKSB series.) Consequently I am now having to let it go and begin packing, even though it really needs me now to sit down with a printed version and read it before sending it off. I will be away for a month...

Much love to you all

BRONWYN

From Susanne 14–9-09

Dear Jonathan, Bronwyn and Ken—sorry for my lack of response to date but I am far away from beginning any new reading path—I am trying now to catch up after hours on several book chapters and papers that are seriously overdue and are excruciatingly difficult to write. At work I am in the other acting admin job and it is sucking phenomenal amounts of time and energy. I've had to drop out of another reading group already. So I'm not ready to read Badiou though the other three of you might be. Don't let me cramp your style. I feel I haven't even caught up enough with Deleuze and the other areas of reading I want to pursue that have emerged from that. If the book is now turning to Badiou you'd be better counting me out at this stage rather than waiting for me to catch up because I'm likely not to. BTW, I have enjoyed reading your messages J and seeing you B but I have been slow to respond because of feeling of inadequacy and lack of time to give proper attention. If you can bear to give me a long rope for a bit longer then I will try to respond when I can. Needless to say I'm writing nothing that I want to or that's lovely right now and my research load seems to have completely evaporated both in and out of hours. Best to you all, hope you are managing life better than I am,

S

From Jonathan 14–9-09

Susanne,

I couldn't countenance your not being part of what we do so from my point of view a long rope is the least I wish to offer you. I'm sad and frustrated on your behalf that you feel so crowded by your various responsibilities and commitments and hope that, before long, you find a way to find the space your soul needs.

With all good thoughts and love,

JONATHAN

From Ken 15–9-09

Dear Susanne, Bronwyn and Jonathan

I feel as if I am cheating a little. I have just opened up my Inbox and found a message from each of you. I am aware of the delay/lack of responses that Bronwyn refers to so I am taking this opportunity to reply to you all at once. There is something in all of your writings to which I feel I can respond so it is good to do it all here.

I have written briefly to Jonathan to say how much I loved the Montjaux piece; like Bronwyn when I read it I felt transported there and the lovely gaps that Jonathan left in his writing to allow us to breathe in the warm air of the mountains and to hear the sound of the birds was intensively electric. I want to write back to that writing. Place and space...I am juggling with my position in relation to those words and I like it.

I remember sitting in the car as we drove from Urbana to Chicago with Tami and Jonathan in the front and Bronwyn and I in the back. I had vaguely heard of Pierre Rivière and Foucault's work on his "case" but Bronwyn's quiet careful description of both, as the boring farmland of Illinois flashed by the window, really captured my imagination and I was captivated...

And that leads me to Susanne's recent message and makes me want to shout "Don't give up!," "Hang in there!." I know that feeling so well and feel that it is so important that we keep up our resistance to those arduous pressures and the demands of day to day faculty life. I think we have some lovely writing already "in the can" and it would be a shame to see that withering through neglect as we all move on in different directions. I have been dipping in and out of Badiou for the last 2 or 3 years and so far I haven't been infected so seriously as I have been with Deleuze: however, it would be great to bring him into our work. I have been reading and making notes on Meillassoux also and through this just feel that there is so much space for us to cultivate these amazing seeds in what we do together.

I have been thinking about my slow response time over the last couple of months and simply realised that I have spent a great deal of time finding my

self in ways other than reading and writing and in ways that are really important to me. I have begun to re-discover laughter, relaxation and a world of sensuality that I had written about but forgotten how to live in.

It has been my children's summer holiday and I have spent lovely times
indulging with them. I have taken time out to be with my friends in ways that
I do less of in the winter; I have been festivalling, camping, swimming, party-
ing and enjoying the richness of my life with them. I have found new relation-
ships and re-kindled a simmering long living one in deep affectionate ways
and...well, now I feel ready to re-visit, re-enter this world that we inhabit here.
Whilst I feel a certain dread about the Autumn as it heralds the end of the summer and the onset of long dark days, I am learning to nurture an ambivalence
about its inevitability because it is also a time of harvest; there are rich pickings
in my garden, the vegetables and the fruit trees, but there are also thoughts, feelings and emotions that are welling up in me which I am beginning to be aware
of and want to live with in ways that will help to sustain me through the winter.

Love

KEN

From Susanne 15-9-09

Dear JKB, thanks for your kindness and forbearance....I am not as bad as I
sounded!! I do really need time though to get on top of things here. I am cheer-
ing for you Ken in your rediscovery of ways of being beyond writing and reading, in sensuality and connection—I aspire too to this....I have had a bit of a
lurking nasty head cold throat thing which has been coming and going and
doesn't help my spirit. Hope you landed happily B,

S

From Bronwyn 15–09-09

Dear JKS

Here I am in Stockholm, after 24 hours in planes and airports. It is 9pm at home,
and early afternoon here. I arrived in Helsinki in the early morning—around
6am—and just marvelled to see again the northern early morning autumn
sky. Such a big sky, a completely different blue from anything I've ever seen at
home. It's a sky that lets me know I've arrived in the other hemisphere of my
life. Stockholm is a city I've been to often, and this hotel, the Columbus, is one
I've stayed in before, and I love it. Nothing modern like a lift here—it was built
in 1780 and served as a brewery and workers' living place, then in 1812, when
Pierre Rivière was a boy, it became the home of the City guards and an early
prison. In 1834, the year before Pierre Rivière murdered his mother, sister and
brother it was a cholera hospital....There is so little in Australia that has this kind

of history, that enables me to imagine some of what was in place in Europe in 1835, so I tend to get really excited about it.

It is amazingly peaceful here. Whatever pain the walls saw in the past seems to be gone. And it's still really summer here—I can hear a lawn mower outside and the thick canopy of leaves outside my window have only the faintest suggestion of yellow.

It was heart-warming to read J and K's affirmation of Sue and of her inclusion in the work we do together. I know too well the way admin positions suck the energy out of you, and leave so little room for creative energy and new thoughts—especially when it involves time-consuming new reading. And Badiou is not an easy read.

I began on his "Theory of the Subject" on the plane and will read it in the in-betweens of this trip. I can see already how I can strengthen the Pierre Rivière paper by drawing on some of his work on the subject. One of the things I love about him is his "bad boy" style–he insists on unexpectedly taking up ideas that have been abandoned, and taking them elsewhere—and he seems to delight in an irreverence toward things "sacred," while at the same time affirming things he might want to knock—like Maoism and Christianity. He turns the subject into an algebraic formula that absolutely makes sense—and I get it even though I was really bad at algebra.

I think it's good if we each read what we can and contribute what we can without feeling any kind of intense pressure about it. I don't want to impose Badiou on you, but I do want to communicate my excitement about what he has to offer. And yes, I don't think I've yet read enough of Deleuze either, so I'm by no means suggesting we abandon him.

24–9-09

I am now in Sundsval, an exquisite small city that has a lot of the beauty of Stockholm, but it takes only 30 mins to walk from one end of it to the other. I sat on the veranda of a summer house today after my lecture and looked out over the sea. This summer house, I learned, is at risk of invasion from minks during the winter. They break in and have babies and feed them fish, so that when the owners return in the spring the house stinks of fish. There was a large fake owl hanging at the edge of the veranda to scare away the birds who poo on the chairs, but it seems the birds are getting used to the owl and are coming in anyway into the shelter of the veranda. From the veranda it is possible to see thick forest on either side, and in front, mirrored sheets of sea water with smooth round rocks and forested islands and absolute quiet. The bears are breeding up in the forest on this particular island so that people now feel afraid to go into the forest. This life of summer houses and close encounters with nature and the extraordinary beauty of the islands and the water and the sun, all inflected with Swedishness, is surprising and endearing and breathtaking all at once. At the end of the month the houses will be closed down for the winter and won't be opened until April. I had a fantasy about being a homeless person and coming to live there for the winter, trying to keep warm by the open fire, sharing my life with minks and bears....It is lovely to get home to my small hotel room decorated like a ship's cabin, and to find your emails waiting for me...

Leaving the university seems now, from this distance, like having broken up an (almost) 40 year marriage. It was the love affair, you could say, that I went into after my other marriage ended.

Much love to you all

B

From Susanne 24–9-09

Dear everyone,

I am waiting for auto electrician to re-gas air conditioning in my car—he forgot me so sent me away for half an hour while he finishes a doc appointment so I will be late for work and snatch a minute. Bronwyn's message of being enveloped in nature (minks, my god!) is just wonderful. The irony is extraordinary. Yesterday, Sydney and all surrounds (and way beyond) were enveloped for more than 24 hours by a thick red dust storm. Up here in the mountains it seemed more yellow than red when I looked out the window at dawn—quite surreal and alien. We are the driest inhabited continent and this was a reminder. I realised I can't stand anymore having broken air-conditioning in my car when it means I have to drive with the window down in conditions like that. I went through the tunnel you used to use to go to work Bronwyn, with the windows down, and felt like I was being poisoned (I guess I was).

The rebound love affair is an intriguing metaphor, always a risky and sometimes toxic undertaking. You sound really wonderful—who would have thought leaving the formal institution would be so academically/ intellectually invigorating. You are setting us a great example of some more ways that a life can be well lived. I am fine. I'm not sure about my normal self, who or what it is...

My brother came for the weekend from a big mine in WA where he drives a big truck and is very happy doing so. We have probably never spent time alone together. We went to see the amazing Circus Oz, to a film, I sent him off riding and surfing. On his last morning he led me through an elaborate and wonderful tai chi like pattern of exercises that he has modified from some karate routines (that are usually fisted and fast but he does them open handed and slow and names each form with its Korean name as he does it). He is such a surprise package—and if his stay had been one day shorter we wouldn't have got to this point. Nor would he have been surprised at my aptitude or my capacity to follow instruction (when I have been tagged in the family as physically inept relative to other sibling sports persons). He taught all sorts of martial arts for decades to children in the small town where he lived. He has all sorts of black belts. He does 30 pushups and 50 situps (or is it the other way around) each lunchtime at work rather than sit around. Despite all this he is quite a gentle guy, as much interested—albeit in his idiosyncratic way—in Buddhist philosophies and practices.

I can't help but recall—every time I look at him because it is etched on his face in a tracery of scars across his eyebrows, chin, mouth—that he almost died when he was 15 when he had an accident as a pillion passenger on a motorbike on a gravel road without a helmet. He had the last rites on the night of the accident and then was in a coma for three months. He is as unlike me as it's possible to be, but the weekend reminded me of how worthwhile it is to grope our ways towards one another across our differences. Also of how much we loved him and feared for him in that awful time (I was in my first semester of first year at uni and they wouldn't let me leave so I went in to the city a few times a week to spend bedside time with him and mum—who lived in a motel near the hospital all that time). Wow. Families. Anyway last night, partly on his compliment of my capacity to do something with my body, I went to an Iyengar yoga school I've just heard about nearby and despite never having done this type and very little of any, it was great and I feel very good today and will try and make it a practice to go to the class. Other fronts like work—can you guess who apparently was #1 publisher at UWS last year? I am amazed and should be pleased but it makes me reflect on the old "life/work balance" cliché. There are a lot of bush tracks I could have been exploring on all those weekends writing... Love to you all, time to go to get the gas (I do feel bad about carbon footprint and CFGs or whatever they are but I can't cope without a/c in this country and in the summer).

xxS

From Jonathan 24–9-09

Dear all,

I had wanted by now to have read your Pierre Rivière paper, Bronwyn, and to have maybe responded to your JKS 15.9.09 writing. I haven't as you can see but wanted you to know that I carry them both with me and will find the space in due course. Susanne, I hope that both your throat and your spirit are in much better shape; and I join you in your cheers for the mighty Ken.

With love,

JONATHAN

From Ken 24–9-09

Dear Everyone (I like that Susanne!)

I have just sat down and read the two messages, one from Susanne and one from Bronwyn. Thank you. I love the sense of place in both your writings and the way in which you brought your brother to us Susanne. He sounds a star! I can do about 40 push ups but all those black belts and karate chops, wow! I know what you mean about looking after your body, it is so easy not to and just jump in the car or relax and watch a film instead of going for a walk. We have had an indian summer here this September and the sea is still really warm (although a lot of my friends disagree with me!). I have a swim in the sea most days if I can. On Friday evening I went to the beach with Reuben and Phoebe and we had a bbq and then just as the high spring tide reached its capacity and the sky was beginning to lose its light we went for a swim. The sea was unusually flat calm and felt heavy, swollen and richly beautiful like a pregnant woman. We just swam and laughed and dived and chased each other and then shivered ourselves dry on the beach in the virtual dark. Walking home in the sandy wet was a delight, listening to the children's animated conversations and feeling tingly all over in mind and body.

I felt something of a shiver thinking of your minks Bronwyn; I'm not sure that I would like to be that close to them. I was convinced I could hear a mouse in my house the other night and it was the most fitful sleep that I had for a week. Where you are in Sweden sounds idyllic Bronwyn and you are there opening up a brand new Deleuze audience; that's great. Perhaps we should try to set up a Deleuze studies retreat there! Their enthusiasm for his work sounds really fresh and invigorating, just like the Swedish countryside you describe in your writing. Something of a contrast to the toxic dystopia that you describe in your car journey Susanne. OMG is it really like that!

I loved the descriptions of France that Jonathan gave us a few weeks ago and feel that it is wonderful the way we bring space in to play so much in our writing. In all three of these pieces there is a telling intensivity which flies beyond the simple description of physical space. Is it right that we can call upon the descriptive or "objective" explanation of extensive space as "place"? (This is Montjaux, this is Sundsvall, this is Sydney, this is Millbrook) but that any description of place must be suffused with our experiential and experiencing selves such that our talk of these places always tends toward the intensive? All your writing about/with these places is so evocative that it seems to me that it can't be anything else. There is also a powerful sense in the way in which you have all written here of the reader being able to read and of being able to enter the spaces to which you refer. I noticed the physicality of Jonathan's writing and the literal spaces that were there for breathing in the lovely images that he offered, living with them for a while in relation to what they evoked in sense, feeling and value.

It was the Autumn Equinox on Tuesday so I am anticipating the onset of dark evenings and shorter days with substantial trepidation. I don't like the winter and the way in which it cloaks everything with sombre tones; looking for life always seems like hard work. But then it is usually a time of writing industry for me; the sea and the beach is no longer there to distract me as much as it does in the summer and spring months and so I resort to my books and the glow of the table lamp reflected in the darkness of my window for contemplative solace.

It is so lovely to hear from you all

love

KEN

From Bronwyn 26–9-09

Dear every one, dear lovely ones, dear loved ones in the JKSB series, dear 5th stream,

I have just spent a couple of hours trying to reconstruct the bits of our writing into one text. J's endnote grabbed some of the text and gobbled it into its own endnote mind and I didn't know how to get it out, and of course I know I have missed some emails. If you see any missing, or if you already have a more complete text, let me know. What putting it all together has done is to open up a lovely space of reading the flows in between us.

I have also spent some hours in free float pondering the week here, and wondering about the de-individualising move that I think is so important.

But first, I have also been struck with the difference, while I'm on this trip, between what I write to you and what I write to others. If I am writing an email to others I keep it as brief as possible on the assumption that the reader wants a clear and to the point message, and that if I ramble on there's a good chance they won't read it and also they won't reply. My messages to others flit over the surface of things and are primarily instrumental and ephemeral. What makes the shift in this writing is the commitment to listening and responding even at the most minute level—not always and to everything—but our words are not treated as ephemeral in the way of email but as having substance to be turned to and returned to, to be threaded together into some as yet unknown fabric. So we fold and unfold the cloth of our writing, we finger it, a bit like I do when I go into a material shop or a clothes shop. I put my hands on the fabric to see how it feels, how it flows. Attracted first by the colour and the shape, I move in close to get the feel of it in my fingers. If it doesn't feel good I have no further interest in it. Later, if I buy it, then the smell and the feel of it on my body will come into play. I will develop a relation between the cloth and my body, it will become part of my body and my body will become part of it. Or maybe not. It might sit in the cupboard until I throw it out or give it away...But our words are the ones for wearing, beautiful sensual words with gorgeous colours, even when we don't know the names of them.

28–09-09
Clouds. Sundsvall in autumn 09.

Blue clear sky fills my eyes
The blank outspace of night
Banished
A simple pulling back of curtains.

Grey clouds gather
The blank page of sky
Overwritten
With oppressive, infinitely shifting letters.

I must get out my raincoat
Fend off the cold air.
Red dust
Yearning for this beneficence.

1–10-09
Dear JKSB, dear lovely ones...
I am sitting in my hotel room in Oslo. I am on the 4th floor and on the wall opposite is a *trompe l'oeil* painting of a narrow road with very old wooden buildings on either side and spring leaves on the trees and vines. The sky is mostly covered in clouds but they are light spring clouds. The actual sky if I go up close to the window and look up, is an autumn sky with fewer clouds. This morning I was woken by the cleaner coming in to do my room at 8.45. He was actually in the room and had started cleaning before he discovered I was asleep in bed. I had been dreaming a long dream about killing my brother Tony, though the dream switched the victim to my husband. For no apparent or immediate reason I had stabbed him in the stomach twice while he was sleeping. The wounds were neat and red, but no blood could be seen pouring out. Anyway, I checked occasionally to see if there was any blood, but I knew he was dead. I needed to continue with my studies so I delayed dealing with the dead body. Now the scene switches to travelling on a train with a young man I barely know and we are in a foreign country. The ticket inspector comes and a young man is found without the right ticket and he is strung up on a rack that is a bit like a crucifixion cross, but at 45 degrees and he is facing down and tied in so we can all see what happens to people who do not get it right. I look at my ticket and see it is not right either. The young man I am travelling with has not

explained the system to me well enough and I should have three dots to punch and I only have one. I begin to explain to the ticket inspector (now a woman) that I have to study, it is very important, and that I have killed my husband and that I did not understand the ticket system as it has not been properly explained to me. She is sympathetic and I begin to weep and weep and weep. She advises me that there are people at the Community Centre who I can ask for help. The scene switches back to Kings Cross, where I live, and I am walking along looking for the community centre and I miss it, and instead come to an open air small police station where a policeman is holding a kid on his knee and playing computer games, and another is sitting idly watching. I tell them I am looking for the community centre where I need to talk to K.M. (a colleague from my days in Townsville many years ago) and they tell me I have walked right past it. I explain I have murdered my husband, and that I have an urgent need to study, and that I have been advised to talk to Kay first before coming to them. They take down the details. The scene shifts. I am looking for the community centre and walk through a bus shelter filled with teenage kids. They start making fun of me, as I am clearly vulnerable and shaken. I walk through feeling terrible, but when I get to the end I turn round and shout at them, don't try to mess with me. I have just murdered my husband, so watch out! They are very quiet and a bit scared. I turn round and keep walking and my walk has changed into a masculine, powerful, slightly swaggering walk. I feel very pleased with myself. The murder has made me strong. I still can't find the community centre. The scene shifts back to the bedroom. The body has been moved. I decide to wash the sheets to remove the evidence. I pull the sheets off and there is still not much blood. The undersheet has much more blood. I pull the mattress out onto the lawn (which is now the back garden of my childhood home) and see that it is full of blood. I cannot imagine how to get the blood out of the mattress. I wash the sheets and undersheet and the blood won't come out of the undersheet. I am feeling deeply vulnerable and afraid. The police will come soon I know and everything will be lost. I have no defence. I keep looking at the mattress full of blood, it is sagging at the bottom with deep pockets of blood, and have no ideas what to do with it. This evidence of blood cannot be destroyed. I worry about my studies and don't know if I can get back to them. I think about the policemen coming. I try to think of a defence I might make in court, but I know there is none. Then I accept that I will be going to jail for a period of time, and in that acceptance feel enormous relief, almost elation. It will be a kind of forgetting. A time out. Time to think, maybe even time to get to my studies...

It was an amazingly vivid dream and could have gone on if the cleaner had not come in on it. Each separate scene was visited a number of times as if it was really important to remember it. The dream clearly follows my earlier dream of Larry, my husband, coming back to kill us all. But it has moved a few steps further. I have become the murderer and I cease being afraid. I of course with my very literal mind want to go to the question of did I really murder my husband ie was it my fault that he could not go on living, but that seems not the point of the dream whose intention is much more metaphorical. It is about the forgetting and letting go that Deleuze advocates, as well as taking responsibility for one's actions and their consequences. It is also about fluids. Is the mattress my body that is full of blood, blood that stubbornly stays in place continuing to live, yet holding the knowledge of the death and the pain of his life, and of our lives together?

Butler quotes Laplanche's words in which he refers to the "irreducible meshing of my death with the death of the other" (Butler, 2005: 75).

And it is also about the urgency of working (studying) in order to open up thought as we are doing now.

The dream is also about the violation of women and of vulnerable young people (such as the violation of Jonathan that he describes in the JK book) I think. It is about being in what Badiou calls the outspace with no chance of recovering one's footing in place, in order to become recognizable as some one, and thus to be recognized. One is positioned as weak, as attackable, and also as an abject other to be punished somehow. Power (violent violating power) can be wielded over the one who has been abjected in the name of keeping the normative/moral order in place. The dream is about that young violated person recovering her own power and losing her fear of the violating forces, and it is also about the enmeshing of the death of one with the other.

In an artwork that I made as part of our work for the book *Pedagogical Encounters*, there are two cuts in the surface layer of cloth and underneath, a large drop of blood. Some saw this art-work of mine as a self-portrait. I hadn't planned it as that, but now, finding again in my dream, the body with two cuts and the blood, supposedly my husband's, I realise this body, these cuts, this blood, is probably also mine.

My fascination with *I Pierre Rivière having slaughtered my mother, my sister, and my brother...* (Foucault, 1975) was sparked more than a decade ago by the possibility of understanding the enactment of extreme violence. I wanted to return to my marriage to understand it from my husband's point of view. Cixous wrote somewhere that for her fiction was a more insightful way of writing, and that such writing should begin with the best known/unknown other. So I began two projects, one writing about Pierre Rivière, and one writing a novel about my husband's life. The latter I gave up on as it generated emotions in my family that seemed too difficult to manage, too dangerous.

B

OF NIGHTMARES AND THE ONTOLOGY OF PLACE

From Jonathan

Bronwyn,

I'm sorry that it has taken me this long to respond to your PR paper. I have many excuses but none of them will quite do, I'm afraid. Busy, certainly. The day job, much of the time, gives me satisfaction and fulfilment but it has recently crowded out writing and the connections that it brings.

So, listening to Pierre Rivière has been a slow pleasure. Thank you so much for sharing it and for asking for feedback. I didn't know the story and didn't know the Foucault edited collection relating to it, but I loved learning about PR, loved being drawn into his painful, painful life and into the issues that surrounded it (and, as you seem to me to infer, still pertain at some level). I loved, too, how you drew Badiou into your piece (and Nancy). I feel that I learned much from your take on Badiou, which is helpful in thinking about how we might use him within our writing. For instance, your explanation of his characterisation of evil at the foot of page 23 struck me hard. I have never seen such a thoughtful definition of evil.

We think we know what it is (sometimes), even if we don't believe that evil exists, but Badiou (or your summary of his position) makes it material. I was drawn in too by your positioning of Pierre Rivière's mother. I had been seduced into seeing her as "bad," but your insights into the way in which she was treated by her husband brought me up, like you, with a jolt.

I wonder: is there value in making any explicit links between this story and now? Might it be contextualised within any one of the number of stories that could be told from contemporary socio-politics of today? I feel that it's powerfully relevant—about how we/nations/societies don't listen, about how we project "evil" into individuals and groups, about how we take up judgement, etc. But maybe it's better being implicit and letting us do the work. Just a thought.

Thank you too for your recent writing to the group from Sundsvall. I hope to be able to re-engage soon.

With love,

Jonathan

From Ken 2–10-09

Dear Bronwyn

Just to say that I have read your recent addition to our writing. I am a bit over-awed and not ready yet to respond other than to say there seems to be so much for me to say. It is so lovely that you can give such intimate and vivid writing to us. I feel excited about the potential that your writing offers to respond, there is so much there. I have been having bad dreams recently but they do not have the duration of yours, they are mainly frightening and scary fragments that wake me and leave me feeling weak and exhausted.

Thank you for your lovely inspiration

love

KEN

From Jonathan 26–10-09

Dear SBK,

How are we? You/we have been on my mind. I have only recently re-engaged with our writing—Bronwyn's from Sweden, in particular, writing to which I have failed so far to respond. I am sorry about this. There have been many immediate and demanding pressures this past month and I have not had the space that I would like for writing. For thinking, even. But still, it feels like not doing due justice to you.

So, I hold you in mind. Sue, under the weight of administrative responsibilities, I imagine; Bronwyn, still travelling perhaps; and Ken, on his way to join me in the north of England at the end of this week when it will be good to be together.

with love,

JONATHAN

PS Bronwyn, did you receive my email in response to your Pierre Rivière paper?

From Bronwyn late October 09

Dear JKS

I too have been wondering how we are, as we've been going through a really silent patch. I have not sent in any more thoughts as I felt strongly the need to leave a space for you three to say something. Jonathan I did get your response to Pierre Rivière, which I really appreciated. I didn't respond immediately as I didn't want to put pressure on Ken and Sue about responding to it—which was pretty silly reasoning, and then the moment slipped away from me while I pondered it....Anyway, yes, I was happy that you had made a kind of sense of what I am trying to do there. That paper will certainly count among the most difficult papers I've ever written. I need to get to the point soon where I can do another good draft of it, and then send it to Jane to get the ball rolling for the Pierre Rivière workshop that she has in mind for next year.

I have just, this morning, got back from 4 days in Newcastle helping my son Paul to paint his new house, and babysitting my grandson Oscar in order to give his parents a break. I have an intense longing just to be at home for a while, having been to Brisbane the weekend before to see Jake (my middle son) and his family, but my youngest son's son keeps emailing me about when I am coming to visit them, and so I can't stay put for long.

It is raining here at the moment, and the air has a real chill on it. A week ago it seemed that summer had arrived. The loveliest thing at the moment, here, as well as in Brisbane and Newcastle, are the jacaranda trees in full bloom. They look at their most spectacular against a dark grey cloudy sky. I wish I could hold the vividness of that colour in my mind's eye forever

Much love to you three.

BRONWYN

Note

1. There is much that we've written of course that is not included. The [cut] here indicates a decision to cut something that was integral to the flow at that point, but that could not be included in the more public space of this book.

Plateau Three

Sea Reflections (JKB)

In which Bronwyn visits Jonathan and Ken. J, K and B reflect on the sea, and on being with others, at home and at sea.

From Jonathan Monday evening, 15 February 2010 Norwich
I left our hotel in Norwich about an hour ago, leaving Tessa there. She's laid up after her surgery last week, having today been more active than any day since the operation. This afternoon, with Joe and his friend Liss (short for Alycia), we drove the forty minutes north (though we could equally have travelled east) to the sea, to a town called Cromer, famous for its crabs. (That's twice in a week that I have walked by the sea, though both times it's been too cold to linger.)

Cromer was drab. Decaying Victorian buildings, a games arcade that was open but empty, and the greyness of the sea itself. The sea was flat, too, with no energy in its waves. We walked only briefly along the front, too short a time for Tessa who wanted to drop down to the beach to look for shells. Joe and Liss walked well ahead, arm in arm, talking fast, while Tessa and I dawdled. Walking was hard for her.

I have enjoyed being with Joe. We spent the afternoon together yesterday, walking around the city, getting a beer and watching a film while Tessa rested. Life is always eventful around him: Yesterday morning we arranged to meet at 11.00am. He texted to say that he would be late and eventually arrived at 11.40am, joining me at Jarrolds' café as I wrote and read Deleuze while Tessa paid homage at the art shops. Joe explained that he had been delayed because he had gone deaf in one ear. The night before, fearing that he would be unable to sleep because of his housemates' noise, he had stuffed his ears with dampened toilet paper. This had succeeded in blocking out the racket but also in giving him a problem in the morning. He was unable to remove the "plug" from one ear and in the attempts to clear it that made him late for meeting us he managed only to ram it in further. When Tessa joined us in Jarrolds and heard the sorry tale, and after we had recovered from our not entirely sympathetic giggles, she purchased tweezers, performed a delicate operation back in our hotel and his hearing was restored to great relief.

So now I'm on my own this evening in a pub, writing, after our afternoon by the sea, while Tessa has a very early night. It took me the hour to find a place to be. My pub selection criteria were: real ale, food, a fire (it's snowing) and open (a basic criterion that my first destination failed, having apparently closed down some time ago). After a significant trek and after dismissing several hostelries because they failed to meet my stringent standards, I found where I am. It's open, the beer is good, the fire roaring (though some distance away) and there is food. The bar staff, two young women, are working furiously and, although the clientele seem friendly and respectful, their patience and good humour are admirable. As I watch them I become curious about their lives. One sounds as if she is from abroad. My guess is that both are students.

Bronwyn's considerations of Butler and Nietzsche have returned to me here. (I've just started to read Foucault properly for the first time. I haven't yet got to Nietzsche.) I've been working on a piece about Deleuze and the counselling work that I do. Deleuze (alone and together with Guattari) is scathing of the psychoanalytic theory and practice that is my first base, however much I have drawn from other perspectives over the years. "Psychoanalysis is the murder of souls," Deleuze writes at one point (Deleuze, 2007: 93), an assertion that is almost gentle in comparison to his comments about Freud and Melanie Klein. I think that Deleuze is wrong about some of his criticism, that he bases it on misunderstandings of notions of the unconscious and of psychoanalytic "interpretation." I'm intrigued about how dismissive he is; similarly to Bronwyn wondering about Judith Butler, I wonder if Deleuze is giving something of himself away in the position he takes. And yet how enriching—and not incompatible with psychodynamics, in my view—are his figures and conceptualisations: to pay attention as a counsellor to the "assemblage" within the consulting room, to be interested in "differenciation" (both the patient's and mine), to be conscious of whether we are—and/or the patient is—in striated space and to look for lines of flight into smooth space, and more, all of these feel to be rich ways of being and thinking within the work. I want to sit with Gilles and ask him whether he realises, despite himself, just how fruitful his ideas are for someone who readily works with psychodynamic thinking. I'm not sure he'd be willing to hear that.

My beer is finished and the snow has stopped so I shall head back to the hotel. When I step out of the pub I shall see the cathedral spire lit up in front of me. I love being here and don't relish returning home tomorrow.

From Bronwyn 19th Feb 2010 Cornwall with Ken

Driving with Viv from Eden. The Cornish light is unlike anything I have ever seen. Today, as the sun descended toward the sea, Viv and I were on our way home to Ken's place, when we noticed the light on the sea and had to pull over. The warm yellow light of the sun barely pierced through the gathered cumulus clouds, and far off out to sea, grey sheets of rain were etched against the white light of the sky. Overhead the sky was overcast, full of water, and the wind coming off the sea was icy cold. The air from our lungs made our own new small clouds with each breath. There was one pool of golden glittering water, far out to sea, just below the sun, that had first caught our attention, and off to the north there were misty slate blue headlands, one in front of the other, vividly outlined against the light grey sky. On the surface of the water at the base of the headlands, and stretching far off out to the distant horizon, was a strip of soft milky white—glowing so intensely that it seemed the sea was literally rising up to meet the sky. Immediately in front of the rising white band of light the sea was alive, playing tricks with our eyes. For a second it would flash deep blue, then fade to light blue, then flash again. And again. I was mesmerised, aware of my toes turning to ice and not caring, not caring for anything but the light and the sun sinking lower, and then the rays of light that pierced through the clouds and descended to the sea. A black bird swooped down from the sky, gliding on the cold air, its outline vividly etched on the blue-whiteness of the sea.

The Tate at St Ives with Ken. We had walked around the exhibitions together, every now and then being taken by surprise when we turned around and realised that the view out the large window was more beautiful than anything we might ever see inside the gallery. When we had finished with the 2 exhibitions, we went up to the fourth floor and into the cafe. We ordered tea and coffee and cakes. And when I looked up, the scene framed by the window was so unexpected it took my breath away. As we had walked about the town the day had passed several times from cloudy and overcast to sunny, and just as we sat down in the café the light suddenly returned. The rooftops were lit up with bright yellow lichen on dark grey slate, the pitched angles of roof-tops like so many deep blue-grey lichen-daubed mussels gathered on rock at the water's edge. In Virginia Woolf's own words, describing St Ives: "The walls were thick blocks of granite built to stand the sea storms. There was nothing mellow about them; no red brick; no soft thatch....It was a windy, noisy, fishy, vociferous, narrow-streeted town; the colour of a mussel or a limpet; like a bunch of rough shell fish clustered on a grey wall together" (Dell and Whybrow, 2003: vii). The wet lichen on slate rooftops, freshly lit by the sun, was improbably bright, improbably beautiful on the grey-blue slate. I looked around, later, in the bookshop for a photo of just that view, thinking it must be a famous view—that is what anyone coming to St Ives must want to see. But no-one had photographed it. Perhaps no-one had ever seen it, just like that, at winter's end, the lichen covering the rooftops, lit by the bright yellow sun at three in the afternoon. If we had come yesterday when it was raining we would have missed it. But then the others in the coffee shop did not seem to have noticed, now I think about it, what was happening in front of their eyes. A middle aged man with his aging mother. A man and wife, the wife burdened with her own bulk, and the 2 teenage children. A family with young children. A young couple. Weary, glad to sit down. Not breath-taken by the view, but pleased perhaps to have the light and a view of some sort. The clouds came over, and the sea turned grey and flat. A small pool of vivid light shone just on the lighthouse. The lighthouse of *To the Lighthouse* (Woolf, 1992). The place of desire for the small boy. The pool of sunlight around the lighthouse lit the white lighthouse, shining white against the surrounding grey, and white crested waves ruffled the rock base of the lighthouse, silent in the distance, benign. Yet signalling danger to sailors—and possible death.

Talland House with Ken. I wanted to go to St Ives because that was where Virginia Woolf had spent her childhood holidays, and where she had based *To the Lighthouse*. I had found on the web that it had been turned into luxury apartments and so had the address. Ken had been there many times but not known of the connection with the Stephen household. The night before we had met in a Cornish pub for a beer with Ken's close friends Martin and Graham, and it turned out Martin had the lovely book on St Ives *Virginia Woolf and Vanessa Bell: Remembering St Ives,* and wanted to lend it to me. With the help of the map in that book we found the street it was in. Large parts of the once grand garden were built out and it was hard to find. A friendly builder working on a stone wall pointed it out to us and took us down the path to find it. And there it was, much as it had been in 1880, but with the top railing on the flat roof now a closed in attic room. I didn't dare trespass into the garden until Ken bravely stepped onto the grass, willing to explore. I walked over to the front of the house and stared at it, imagining the life that had been there with all the children and the many literary and artistic visitors, and servants, all revolving around grumpy old Lesley Stephen. The luminous girls, Stella and Vanessa and Virginia, learning about beauty and grace, right here, learning to write and paint outside the rigid striations of Victorian London. When I turned around from the front of the house to look at the view I was stunned by its beauty. The white lighthouse stood far out on the vivid blue sea, white waves crashing around it. The light on the water made the blue of the sea luminous; not bright and glaring, not glittering, but swelling with light; a vivid blueness filled with winter light. After a while standing there with no-one telling us to leave, we became even more daring, and explored what was left of the garden with its natural spring and pools and green grass and old trees in their winter bareness. They spent months here each summer for the first 12 years of Virginia's life—until her mother died. What grief to lose a mother and this place at the same time; housebound in London with a crazy old grieving father.

We made our way down to the water's edge and found a coffee shop where we could sit in the sun and gaze out over the beach to the sea. Then Barbara Hepworth's beautiful studio and sculpture garden; fresh fish and mussels in wine sauce in a café looking over the sea; the Tate and the sea again; finally walking back through narrow winding cobble stone streets to find the car and wind our way back to Millbrook and the busyness of children arrived home and Viv and Molly about to arrive, and dinner to prepare.

I've just read Jonathan's lovely Norwich writing. I can't quite put my finger on exactly how it is so different now I have spent time staying with each of Jonathan and Ken, to receive this writing. It feels as if I occupy the space of the writing differently. Now I know Tessa, for example, I can see her, and I know her tiredness after the operation, both from hearing it from her and from remembering my own recent day surgery. And although I haven't been to Norwich, I've walked with Jonathan and Tessa through Oxford, and with Ken through the streets here and in St Ives, so walking together with Tessa, with Jonathan, is in my body, and I am in my imagination with them, walking along the old English streets. But more I've been walking by the sea with Ken a lot in the last 2 weeks, and though the sea here is far from drab, I see myself bringing Cromer to life through walks with you both.

I admire J's search for the right place to drink and eat and write. I failed dismally in that when I was in Prague, but the pavements were so treacherous and the bars so smoky. It was easier to stay in. I know from what Ken wrote while I was in Prague that he too, like Jonathan, would have sought just the right place. Maybe, it just occurred to me, there is also some hesitation left over from my early days when women could not go into bars in Australia, and single women still do not really go to bars unless they are looking to pick someone up. I am envious of the freedom you each have in going out in a new city to find the right ale and food and warm fire for writing.

I am intrigued and curious about the discussion on Deleuze and counselling and psychotherapy that J has opened up. I want to hear more. I look forward to reading what you are writing on this Jonathan. It's interesting how often people say collective biography is therapeutic isn't it, in light of this overlap between what Deleuze gives us, and what enables us to live well? In fact I would say Deleuze undoes a lot of what traps us into living badly/unhappily/miserably/destructively—whatever we do that leads us to need a different kind of guidance in putting ourselves together in a way that works. What Deleuzian language would you/could we use to make the contrast I just tried to make I wonder? How might we frame the therapeutic act as a Deleuzian one. I like the start you made here with assemblages and striations and lines of flight, but what language would we ditch and what keep and why in the psychodynamic framework? It is a really interesting question. I'd like to be provoked into thinking about this a lot more deeply. It seems a really rich vein of inquiry.

I am feeling very sad that this time spent with you both is about to end. Tomorrow I am off to Dublin. My washed clothes are drying by the fire. Ken has a marvellous clothesline that works with a pulley to send the clothes high into the windy sky, but even then it is too cold usually for the clothes to dry completely. Viv and Ken are cooking the dinner. Phoebe is just about to come home from a big performance with the girl scouts in Truro cathedral. Reuben is having a sleepover with friends at his Mum's place. Molly is happily curled up somewhere. Music is playing. In Dublin and then in Bristol I will be re-commencing my solitary existence, though with more than enough adventures lined up to keep me happy.

In London I got sucked back into the whole UWS drama. I accepted an adjunct professorship and then the university tried (and momentarily succeeded) to draw me back into all the hideous dynamics I had left behind. I had to do all the emotional work of letting go again, but this time with J's wise counsel. While I've been here in Cornwall UWS has seemed very remote and far away, its power to hurt gone. I hope it will stay that way. I've remembered all over again how lucky I am to be free of all the institutional pressures that had come to weigh so heavily on me. But the grief, I suppose, is not inconsequential.

From Ken. From Cromer to St. Ives—February 2010

I am not sure where to start therefore I will start.

The a priori structure of this sentence is intended. There is no contingency here.

Bronwyn left my house an hour or so ago. I have been sitting in my office for a large part of this time reading Jonathan's "Norwich" writing and Bronwyn's "Cornwall" writing. This sentence tells of how much is there that I feel that I have to write to/with/about.

I don't know where to start.

As is often the case I will start with the sea. I will start with St. Ives and the visit that Bronwyn and I made there and which she refers to in her lovely piece of writing about coming to visit me here in Cornwall. As she says, I have been to St. Ives many times before; there are so many things that I could write about the time I have spent there but our visit last Wednesday was rich with its own stories.

We walked, quietly. Sometimes our walking would be halted by a sense of awe. The glow from the yellow lichen on the rooftops in the purity of the sun-shining *plein air* took my breath away. The turn that Bronwyn describes us tak-ing in Virginia Woolf's childhood garden to see Godrevy lighthouse glowing in the bright, fizzing transparency of pure Cornish light nearly bowled me over.

Sometimes we talked, pointed things out or simply smiled at the shared sense of the raw beauty of it all. My imagination raced: it always races when I find myself immersed in the rough sensuality of the land that I love. I can't help seeing old fisherman everywhere, devout preachers walking from the chapels and girls in heavy long skirts sorting fish on the quay-side. I swim in this world of fantasy and dreams. I want to drink pints with dissolute miners in the heady swirl of the shadowy, dark pubs and talk with the old men smoking and leaning against the stacks of empty crab pots. I know that Bronwyn was moved by her walk in Virginia's garden and there was for me too something uncan-ny, something touching to feel myself there looking up at the tall windows and the cast iron mouldings of the verandah, knowing that she had looked out with wonder from this beautiful spot. It was new for me. I didn't know that as a young girl Virginia Woolf had come to live here in St. Ives with her family and I felt a great desire to chase the will o' the wisp of this seductive story and weave it into the ones that I already have dancing around my head. I think of D. H. Lawrence and Frieda, of Ben Nicolson and Barbara Hepworth, of Patrick Heron and all the "foreigners" that the often xenophobic Cornish would treat with suspicion and contempt. I think of my own love of the "character" of the Cornish, for me so significantly embodied in the miners, the fisherman, the farmers and the rugby players all of whom have filled my life with joy over the years as I have travelled the land. I love to bring these Cornish sensibilities of mine into contact with the painting, the poetry, the sculpture and the writing that people from the "outside" seem to have brought with them then refined and re-grown in the wild, heady richness of this strange once isolated world. It made me laugh to think of the locals being annoyed and complaining, as yet another of Barbara Hepworth's massive completed sculptures would block the narrow streets of the town as it was moved from her studio to generate fame, wonder and fortune in some exotic location on the other side of the world.

I feel this ambivalence in me as I try to paint pictures with my words. I think of the tough, practical and sometimes austere ways that were nurtured in me in my Cornish childhood. I smile at the contrasts and the complexities of this life as I find myself drawn into the webs of intrigue surrounding Lawrence's life on the cliffs above Zennor, or of Virginia Woolf's childhood dreams as she looked out from her garden to the Godrevy light. I love the fierce colour of Terry Frost's abstracts, the manic Dada energy of Kneehigh Theatre and the sombre realist beauty of Stanhope Forbes' fish market.

I think of Jonathan's grey sea and live with a strong sense of knowing as he sits there in the pub, writing, distracted by the people there, drawn in by their character and the vibrancy of their life, writing always writing. I contrast the grey sea of the east coast with the seething colours of Wednesday's St. Ives sea, both bathed in and generating this iridescent Cornish light. I am immersed in the wonder of our writing together. I smile at the productive desire that takes us from these moments of sensual pleasure to our keyboards. I tingle with the sense of love and beauty that takes my imaginings of Cornish life and folds them into the flaming rush of energy that the thoughts and ideas that I am having now generate. I dance with these curiosities and complexities and feel so warm and privileged to be able to live these moments with you in these fickle words.

From Bronwyn 22–02-10 Maynooth in Ireland

It's curious isn't it that so much of our writing takes place when we are not "at home." Deleuze thought travel was generally a bad thing, but for us it seems to open up not just the chance of writing, but the liminal space in which we can think *other-wise*. Other-wisdoms. Becoming-other. When we are away, sometimes, the repetitions of daily life halt, and a space of other knowing is opened up. When J wrote that he loved Norwich and didn't look forward to going home, I was surprised and not surprised at the same time. Having just been with him "at home," and simultaneously myself away from home and seeing everything vividly with the freshness and surprise of new space, I couldn't at first imagine it as a place he might not want to be. Norwich presented J with something of what his "at home" presented me with. "Home" may be a safe plot of land, but it is also the place of endless repetitions, of circling back upon the same problems, a place in which old anxieties lodge themselves in the cracks, and accumulate with the dust; with the dry, shed skin of life.

There is someone I don't know living in my apartment at the moment, only for a few days I think. I chose not to rent it while I was away, because I thought the anxiety of having my space taken over by someone else would be unbearable. I couldn't bear to think of their dirt in my space, of their spilling their wine and greasy food on my carpet, their shed skin accumulating in my bed....(I'm really aware of shed skin as I travel, since the air is so cold and so dry I am losing layers and layers of it—*and* shedding it in other people's spaces). But a week ago an email popped into my box, asking if someone who goes to my café, "a woman with long grey hair and a long coat," whom I've seen but never talked to, could have it for a few days, and I said yes. She will let in fresh air by opening my windows. She is using her own sheets. I have been away long enough now, it seems, to allow her sojourn in my space to pass without too much anxiety.

I have been travelling for almost 6 weeks. I will be on the move for another 10. Perhaps I'm getting the hang of travelling, as I feel less anxious than I usually do. But then everyone is taking such good care of me that I can't help but feel like J in Norwich, that being away from home is good.

Dublin and Maynooth are surprising. I haven't been to Ireland before, and I am taken by surprise by how familiar it seems. There has been a lot of Irish migration to Australia; almost 40% of Australians are of Irish descent, and many of my friends and ex-students have Irish ancestors; there is something too of our histories that are similar—a relationship with England as a colonising power and, until quite recently, not secure in our own separate identities. The huge difference between Ireland and Australia is the monolithic power of the Catholic church here. There is no choice here; the church runs the schools, the families, the communities and god knows what else. At home, even for those born into strong Catholic families, it is possible to imagine existing outside the church.

Last night I stayed in a castle in Dublin, and tonight I am in the Bishop's suite on campus in Maynooth. At the grand driveway to the seminary is the remnant of an ancient castle. The seminary was designed by a famous architect, Pugin I think, and it is indeed very beautiful. 250 young men each year used to enrol to become priests there (today it is more like 10 a year). There is a magnificent church that was built during the famines. (How could such extravagance have been justified at such a time?) Nearby is a statue of one of the Popes. He is sitting and bending down and whispering into the ears of two kneeling children whose heads are bowed and that he is fondling. It makes me feel claustrophobic and sick. It is disgusting, but there seems no way of removing it. "There is no alternative" makes its own kind of sense here. In that way I know I am not "at home" even while I feel very much at home with the people I've met here. I feel myself expanding into the space they create, feeling really happy in that space. There is no perceivable gap between us. I find myself loving their Irish accents and strangely annoyed when there are other accents in the restaurants I've been to. Having grown up Anglican, with Scottish, Welsh and English ancestry, I've always thought somewhere in the back of my mind that I was specifically not-Irish, but the Irishness of Australians has obviously seeped into me without me even knowing it. And of course we share being Celts, in revolt against English colonialism and imperialism.

Today and tomorrow I'm running a collective biography workshop all day and on Wednesday I'm teaching a collective biography masterclass. The cold I developed in the last days at Ken's has given me a shocking cough that takes me over to such an extent that I have to leave the teaching space and retreat to the toilets while the coughing fit subsides. My voice keeps threatening to vanish altogether. I'm just praying that it doesn't disappear completely. I've got a public lecture on Thursday in Dublin. My larynx is my most vulnerable organ. Oh for a body without organs! Once when I was supposed to give the annual lecture in memory of my friend Carolyn I lost my voice. I wrote out the lecture in three voices and had 3 friends of Carolyn's read the parts. They did it well and I was there while they did it, managing the visuals. But some said it was as if I wasn't there, since I *am* my voice. Somehow bodily presence and one's thoughts read out loud do not amount to presence.

My worst fear became evident as the night progressed. This morning I woke with no voice, despite telling myself that overnight I would recover. I ran the collective biography with writing and whispers. The stories and the analytical work that the participants did were amazing. I found myself deeply connected to their stories. It was deeply moving. I've cancelled the masterclass and the lecture—since they cannot be managed with no voice. I feel abject in relation to that giving up on the promise to do them.

I forgot to say how interesting that wet toilet paper cuts out sound. I wonder if I will be tempted to try it next time my neighbours are ramping it up? As long as I have a friend with tweezers...

11–04-10

I have returned to St Ives and the sea and am sitting on Porthminster Beach. It is the beach below Talland house, which you can see from the garden. This is where the children loved to swim. I am staying in a hotel that is almost next door to Talland House, and from my room I share the same view. I have been to the garden this morning and taken photos, and I'm re-reading *To the Lighthouse*. There is a coffee shop here on the beach and I am sitting rugged up against the cold wind, reading and intermittently gazing at the beach and the sea. I quickly scribble notes in the back of the novel, feeling as if these ephemeral images will vanish if I do not write them down.

The whiteness of the large gull drifting on the air makes the sky more blue, the curved stone archway through the headland for the train, the cold air, and the white wall of Talland house, blinding white against the purple clematis. It is September in *To the Lighthouse*, and I am here in April. An ageing woman's face and body, and the lighthouse on the horizon. The track to the beach, not a sandy track through paperbark forest, but granite steps cut square, a sealed pathway, down, through a dense arch of English shrubs and flowers. The sound of the waves, too cold for swimming, last night dumpers churning up the sand and carrying it in huge swathes out to sea. The danger of the water and the waves, and the longing for it, and the crying of gulls drifting on the air. Woolf writes of sand-dunes but there are none. She calls it the Hebrides, but it is St Ives.

The co-implication of Mr and Mrs Ramsay. They give each other meaning. The sea aquamarine on the shore turning to deep cerulean blue dotted with red and yellow buoys. A child with a red bucket on the sand, another with a red hat. Bodies mostly black outlined against white sand except for the splashes of vivid red. White waves and drifts of feathered white clouds. Some boys running at the edges of the water, leaping, daring the coldness. Sadness, and the endless repetition of the waves. The archway punched through the headland, and gulls drifting, arcing, hovering, calling—flap of wings, swoop, drift. Boys in wetsuits now, daring the waves.

Ethics (JB)

In which Jonathan and Bronwyn extend their thinking about, and practice of, a Deleuzian ethics. Deleuze makes a strong distinction between morality and ethics and Bronwyn opens up this space by turning to other writers on ethics to assist in this new thinking about ethics, including Badiou, Bergson and Nancy. Into the space of this thought about ethics she tells the story of her marriage, challenging herself and Jonathan to practice ethics rather than moral judgement.

From Bronwyn 22–03–10

Deleuze distinguishes between morality and ethics, and he opposes the kind of morality that argues from an idealized essence, and that presumes to judge and find wanting those who cannot realize this imposed essence in its perfection:

> Even if man is in essence a reasonable animal [as Aristotle claims], he does not cease to behave in an unreasonable way. How does that happen? It is because the essence of man, as such, is not necessarily realised. Why? Because man is not pure reason, and then there are accidents, he doesn't cease being diverted. The whole classical conception of man consists in inviting him to agree with his essence because this essence is like a potentiality, which is not necessarily realised, and morality is the process of the realization of the human

essence. Now, how can this essence which is only potential, be realized? By morality. To say that it is to be realized by morality is to say
that it must be taken for an end. The essence of man must be taken
for an end by existing man. Therefore, to behave in a reasonable way,
i.e. to carry out the essence is the task of morality. Now the essence
taken as an end is value. Note that the moral vision of the world is
made of essence. The essence is only potential, it is necessary to realize the essence, that will be done insofar as the essence is taken for
an end, and the values ensure the realization of the essence. It is this
ensemble which I would call morality. (Deleuze, 1980)

In contrast to a morality that judges in terms of an external value, an imposed
essence, Deleuze seeks an ethics that is about the powers we have, singly and
collectively, to endure and to engage in creative evolution.

In order to open up the creative forces that enable us to evolve beyond the
fixities and limitations of the present moment Deleuze suggests we turn our
attention to what we are made of, not an essence that should be realised, but
our material continuity and ontological co-implication with others, including
non-human others. He invites us to open ourselves to multiplicity, while decon-
structing the sacralization and ascendance of humanity.

Our writing is, in a Deleuzian sense, not a moral tale, but an ontology, a
lived ethics. Whereas morality involves judgement of the other, ethics rests on
openness to the other and the possibility of oneself becoming different, of
coming to know and to be differently:

Morality is the system of judgment. Of double judgment, you judge
yourself and you are judged. Those who have the taste for morality are those who have the taste for judgment. Judging always
implies an authority superior to Being, it always implies something
superior to an ontology. It always implies one more than Being, the
Good which makes Being and which makes action, it is the Good
superior to Being, it is the One....In an ethics it is completely different, you do not judge....Somebody says or does something, you do
not relate it to values. You ask yourself how is that possible? How
is this possible in an internal way? In other words, you relate the
thing or the statement to the mode of existence that it implies, that
it envelops in itself. How must it be in order to say that? Which manner of Being does this imply? You seek the enveloped modes of existence, and not the transcendent values. It is the operation of
immanence. (Deleuze, 1980)

In such an ethics, the realization of one's identity, through establishing the moral values with which to judge oneself and others, is not the point. The point is to become different from ourselves, to evolve creatively in the space that we open up between and among us. We do so through exploring the infinite multiplicities of being that become possible in that space of Being. We do not demand of each other that we become the completed being that some imagined essence would suggest one should become; we do not impose, from a superior vantage point a definition of Being that presumes to judge and find lacking; rather we seek the opening up of the as yet unknown. That is a commitment, in Bergson's terms, to creative evolution and thus to life itself.

Our nomadic engagement with each other in the writing of this book I would characterise as creative evolution; through an elaboration of moments of being, haecceities were experienced. A mode of being was opened up through which our co-implication in each other as facets of Being was made possible in the very moments of specificity that were brought to life in the writing; in the movement between one and the other life evolved. Our univocity was not generated in the multiplication of concepts as it was for Deleuze, but in the multiplication of moments. These were moments in which we could not be categorised or pinned down, but moments of being that opened up the not-yet-known through the intensities and flows in-between.

When I think about "ethics" as it is relevant to what we have been doing here, I am not talking about the concept of *ethics* that has been appropriated and distorted by "ethics committees" within neoliberalised universities. What goes under the name of ethics there bears little relation to what Deleuze calls *ethics*. What ethics committees do is more like risk-management, or a set of practices that provides the grounds for a legal defence against any research participant who might later claim to have been violated in some way.

Badiou's (2002) analysis of ethics distinguishes between this familiar institutionalised ethics, which he names *contemporary ethics*, and an ethic of truths. He sees contemporary, institutionalised ethics as a reaction against the radical changes that began in the 60s. His analysis of it is that it is embedded in the rationalities of "humanitarian individualism," in which human rights, loosely linked to "public opinion" presupposes a "universally recognizable human subject possessing 'rights' that are in some sense natural....These rights are held to be self-evident, and the result of a wide consensus. 'Ethics' is [understood as] a matter of busying ourselves with these rights, of making sure that they are respected" (Badiou, 2002: 4). He observes that many intellectuals have been won over by the self-evident logic of this humanitarian individualism, and take for granted its embeddedness in capitalist economies and parliamentary democracies. "In so doing," he observes, "they have inspired a violently reactionary movement against all that was thought and proposed in the 1960s" (2002: 5).

Contemporary ethics, in this analysis, is intrinsically conservative and regulative. It loses sight of, and overrules, the particularity and situatedness of ethical *practice*. It begins with the assumption of an a priori evil such as violence and suffering, and imposes a defensive ethics based on "human rights." Underlying those contemporary ethics discourses is a world that is no longer a world, but an economy, an economy that is designed to exploit the "'margin-alized,' 'excluded' or 'Third World' victim, to be protected by a dutiful, efficient, and invariably 'Western' benefactor/exploiter)" (Hallward, 2002: xiii), whose exploitation is to be rendered invisible by the appearance of protection. This approach to ethics has become part of the institutional apparatus through which risk is managed and "ethics" mandated. To find a line of flight away from it is a complex task, and Badiou's analysis helps to make visible the philosophical underpinnings of it, that have made it seem like an unquestion-able common-sense, one that cannot be argued with. Contemporary ethics has, he says, two philosophical underpinnings: "a (vaguely Kantian) univer-salising pole...grounded in the abstract universality of 'human' attributes or rights. And second, a (vaguely Lévinasian) differentiated pole, attuned to the irreducible alterity of the Other" (Hallward, 2002: xiii). On the surface, what it produces is protection of the weak from abusive interference; the research par-ticipant becomes, by definition, a "fundamentally passive, fragile and mortal entity...a potential victim to be protected" (Hallward, 2002: xiii).

And what is wrong with that one might ask. The problem such an ethics brings with itself is that it forecloses the line of flight that enables us to imag-ine ourselves other-wise, to imagine the research participants outside the cat-egories they have been enclosed in. They become the objects of the researcher's gaze, a gaze that fixes them in a common-sense emplacement of vulnerability; a vulnerability in stark contrast to the researcher's power to know. Their irre-ducible alterity, their difference, is set in place by the categorisation of them as *this* kind of person from *that* kind of background. Such categorisations place the other as discrete and distinct from the self of the researcher, with the difference lying in the Other.

Badiou poses an ethic of truths, as an alternative to contemporary ethics. An ethic of truths does not work from categorical difference, but similar to a Deleuzian process of differenciation, is an active process of opening oneself and others to the not-yet-known. This ethic of truths is situated and specific, focused on *events*, on happenings, which implicate everyone "regardless of interest or privilege, regardless of state-sanctioned distinctions" (Hallward, 2002: xiv). In order to remain ethical, subjects caught up in such events, where the world is in process of becoming a different place, must maintain a constant balance between their self-interest in a particular situation, and informed disinterest, which requires of them an openness to other opinions, and other commitments. An ethic of truths does not attempt to impose itself on everyone; it is open to the multiplicity of placements in the world; it will not impose an absolute truth on others, and it will not base its judgements on its own self-interested position (Badiou, 2002: 85).

Nancy (2007b) picks up on a similar difference between current day globalised or neoliberal "ethics" management, and an ethical practice that he calls *world-making*. Globalization, or globe-making, in his analysis, produces over-regulated practices focussed on the production of generic, predictable individuals, responsive to the forces of capital and of government. It is geared to forging docile bodies, bodies "that may be subjected, used, transformed and improved" (Foucault, 1977: 136). Globe-making dismantles the social in favour of the economic.

"World-making," in contrast, is the ethical practice that begins not with the management of others, and of individual identities, but with self-in-relation to the other. World-making entails openness to new directions and possibilities, not mandated by governmental imperatives, but emergent from the specificity of particular places and spaces in the world. It focuses on engagement with the other, where other includes human, non-human, and earth others, and it focuses on anticipating the eruption of the new. It has an unpredictable appearance, maintaining a crucial reference to the world as a space of relationality and as a space for the construction and negotiation of meaning. Against the disembodied and dislocated "everywhere and anywhere" of the global, Nancy (2007b) emphasizes the specificity of subjects in their particular time and space–of "this place, here." World-making, in contrast to globe-making, is not focused on controlling the future. Its question is, rather, how can we give ourselves, open ourselves, in order to look ahead of ourselves, where nothing is yet visible.

The ethics that we have been practicing with Deleuze is akin to Nancy's world-making. For Deleuze, ethics is embedded in a philosophy of immanence, of being-in-itself, where there is no absolute value, or being, that lies outside the Being of which we are all part, in which we are co-implicated in a creative evolution that is "radically heterogeneous; certainly it is biological, but it is also psychological, cultural, geological, oceanic, and meteorological" (Wilson, 2004: 69). There is no place in such world-making from which we might categorise and judge others. Those categorisations that divide us from each other, are a negation of being, and a negation of creative evolution. We are caught up, all of us, all forms of being, of matter, in movement and in change. Although we exist in our singularity, we are all, animate and inanimate beings, integrally caught up in Being.

Deleuze was inspired by the work of Bergson, who wrote in 1911 "what we do depends on what we are; but it is necessary to add also that we are, to a certain extent, what we do, and that we are creating ourselves continually...for a conscious being, to exist is to change, to change is to mature, to mature is to go on creating oneself endlessly" (Bergson, 1998: 7). Creative evolution is not just the province of exceptional individuals, but of all matter. Bergson writes:

> The universe *endures*. The more we study the nature of time, the more we shall comprehend that duration means invention, the creation of forms, the continual elaboration of the absolutely new....[I]n the universe itself two opposite movements are to be distinguished..., "descent" and "ascent." The first unwinds a roll ready prepared. In principle, it might be accomplished almost instantaneously, like releasing a spring. But the ascending movement, which corresponds to an inner work of ripening or creating, *endures* essentially, and imposes its rhythm on the first, which is inseparable from it. (Bergson, 1998: 11)

Contemporary ethics in its rule-following risk-avoiding strategies is like the descending, already known roll that unwinds. An ethic of truths, or a Deleuzian ethics, requires an immersion in the not-yet-known, participating in that which ripens and creates, not controlled and willed by the individual researchers through pre-specified plans, but open to what is already there, that impinges on them and enables them to ripen through coming to know differently. It involves a willingness to take risks, to be open to emergent Being.

In Bergson's philosophy the individual is never perfect, never able to be isolated:

> ...it is often difficult, sometimes impossible, to tell what is an individual, and what is not, but...life nevertheless manifests a search for individuality, as if it strove to constitute systems naturally isolated, naturally closed....Like the universe as a whole, like each conscious being taken separately, the organism which lives is a thing that *endures*. Its past, in its entirety, is prolonged into its present, and abides there, actual and acting. (1998: 15)

Although we may be attached to the accomplishment of our individual identities, we are always much more than our present conscious, intentional selves. We are each co-implicated in Being; we each contribute our voices to the clamour of Being.

Bergson focussed on the limitations of cognition, of categorical thought, and of the presumption that we can see into the essence of things. He understood these as limiting the possibilities of Being that might open up if we could only think otherwise:

> Our reason, incorrigibly presumptuous, imagines itself possessed, by right of birth or by right of conquest, innate or acquired, of all the

essential elements of the knowledge of truth. Even where it confess-
es that it does not know the object presented to it, it believes that its
ignorance consists only in not knowing which one of its time-hon-
oured categories suits the new object. In what drawer, ready to
open, shall we put it? In what garment, already cut out, shall we
clothe it? Is it this, or that, or the other thing? And "this," and
"that," and "the other thing" are always something already conceived, already known. The idea that for a new object we might have
to create a new concept, perhaps a new method of thinking, is
deeply repugnant to us. The history of philosophy is there, however, and shows us the eternal conflict of systems, the impossibility of
satisfactorily getting the real into the ready-made garments of our
ready-made concepts, the necessity of making to measure. (Bergson,
1998: 48)

Deleuzian philosophy picks up this challenge to generate new concepts to
enable us to think outside the limitations of what we already know, to think otherwise, to engage in lines of flight, to move toward difference in oneself, to difference as continuous, to difference that does not separate us off from each other
but "refers to intensities, and to evolution rather than succession" (Massey,
2005: 21).

Working on a plane of immanence, where being is within the thing itself,
and where all things, including all subjects, are co-implicated in each other,
Deleuze does not divide thinking from the material body and from affect, nor
divide the individual subject off from the other. He seeks as writer/philosopher
to open up thought and thus to open up being to change. He sought to think
beyond the individualized subject whose being was sacralised and placed at
the centre of things, toward an embodied Being co-implicated in other forms
of being, where all Being is both material and sacred. Each specific being, in his
philosophy, is infinite in its possibilities. He draws on Spinoza's modes of
existence, or manners of Being, to elaborate this position. "The beings (*étants*)
or what exists (*existants*) are not Beings (*êtres*), there is Being only in the form
of absolutely infinite substance" (Deleuze, 1980).

In this way of thinking, if we are to engage in ethical practices, we each
have an obligation, in relation to our own substantive experience of Being to
work within ourselves in the spaces opened up in relation to other aspects or
experiences of Being, We can explore the specificity of Being as it happens in
its unfolding, infinite multiplicity, rather than impose from outside of itself an
idea or an essence against which it must always fail. Our task is to multiply the
zones of bodily intensity not as individuals, but as manifestations of Being:

> It's not a question of being this or that sort of human, but of becoming inhuman, of a universal animal becoming—not seeing yourself as some dumb animal, but unravelling your body's human organization, exploring this or that zone of bodily intensity, with everyone discovering their own particular zones, and the groups, populations, species that inhabit them. (Deleuze, 1995: 11)

Such a conception of ethical practice takes me, again, to listening, listening both to oneself and to the other, listening not just for meaning, but for affect, for modes of existence that include and go beyond rationally acquired knowledge (Nancy, 2007a). Such listening is not categorical and self-referencing but involves listening to thought with an openness of mind, with openness to differenciation. In Readings' (1996: 165) words:

> *Listening to Thought* is not the spending of time in the production of the autonomous subject (even an oppositional one) or of an autonomous body of knowledge. Rather, to listen to Thought, think beside each other and beside ourselves, is to explore an open network of obligations that keeps the question of meaning open as a locus of debate. Doing justice to Thought, listening to our interlocutors, means trying to hear that which cannot be said but that which tries to make itself heard.

Turning to the nightmares. When we were writing the emails that now form Plateau 2, there were two nightmares that I told in which "the monster" returned and in which he was killed off. The killing of the monster seemed to induce a silence, an end to the flow in between, though there were many other impingements on our time and attention that drew us away. In a Deleuzian ethics, the categorisation of my ex-husband as monster, even in the realm of dreams, can be opened to question. I want to return, now, to those nightmares and see how it might be possible to practice a Deleuzian ethics. I want to ask of my deceased husband, with Deleuze, with Jonathan, "how is that possible? How is this possible in an internal way?" (Deleuze, 1980).

   If someone has come to register, as he did, as fearful monster in my dreams, I might ask, with Deleuze, how is that monster co-implicated in myself? Is his death also my death, our death? I would approach him not with judgement, declaring his murderous intent and his violence toward his wife and children as some kind of personal failure, but with the question "how is that possible"? Is it possible to imagine being this other as collective biography invites us to do? Is it possible to open up an encounter with him as one who inhabited a material specificity, one with specific powers, who existed in an historically specific space that enabled some of those powers to flourish, and closed down others—while at the same time understanding him to be co-extensive with us in the realm of Being? Can we ask not so much who was he, but what could he do/know? What mode of existence was he enveloped in? Can we ask how must it have been to be him, to say and do what he said and did, not attempting to explain, but to know differently in being exposed to him? Is it possible to withhold judgement, and to enter into an ethics that recognizes his ontological co-implication in our lives?

I have wanted to write this story from my husband's point of view for a long time—ever since reading Cixous's advice about beginning from the best-known unknown thing:

> We go toward the best known unknown thing, where knowing and not knowing touch, where we hope we will know what is unknown. Where we hope we will not be afraid of understanding the incomprehensible, facing the invisible, hearing the inaudible, thinking the unthinkable, which is of course: thinking. Thinking is trying to think the unthinkable: thinking the thinkable is not worth the effort. Painting is trying to paint what you cannot paint and writing is writing what you cannot know before you have written: it is preknowing and not knowing, blindly, with words. It occurs at the point where blindness and light meet. (Cixous, 1993: 38)

My husband, who died when I was 25, was, for me, that best-known/unknown other. This desire to write his story as far as I could from his point of view has been difficult for my sons; it is potentially dangerous territory for them and for me. So I do not go lightly into this tale.

Let me begin then with the boy, Laurie. He was born in Sydney in 1939. His father had migrated to Australia in 1930 from a remote Greek village where his family were blacksmiths. He had acquired very little English. His mother, Janet, much younger than George, had Scottish parents and worked as a psychiatric nurse. Laurie was the second child. He found himself in his first years left very much alone with his brother Georgie. His father owned a café that required both parents to work long hours. The father allowed the mother to visit her two babies once every four hours for half an hour. They were otherwise left alone in a dark room at the back of the café. She didn't see them learn to crawl or walk.

In time George and Janet and the two boys left the city in search of land and a new life. They bought a small farm. Once again, the father required endless labour on the part of the mother. He could not bear to see her idle. If she spent time with the children it seemed to him an unbearable form of idleness. When the father did not get his way, his rage was spectacular. Sometimes grabbing the lintel of the doorway above him he smashed his head, repeatedly, against it. It was a fearful thing to witness.

Laurie was an engaging and attractive child, with dark brown eyes and a mop of curly brown hair. His mother adored him. He shared her love of numbers and her shyness. One day she could bear the isolation and fear on the farm no longer and fled, with Laurie, to her mother's home in the city. When George came visiting with Georgie, he appeared contrite, and asked no more than time to be with the two boys to let them play together. He took them for a walk and disappeared.

A year later, when they saw her again at the first court hearing for the divorce, they shrank behind their father, apparently afraid of her. She opened up her arms to them, calling out their names "Laurie! Georgie!" But they would not come to her.

Her lawyer pointed out that she would never gain custody if the magistrate saw their fear.

She cancelled the proceedings, and returned to the marriage. They sold the farm and moved back to the city. George had a dog that lived in the small back yard behind the new shop. The dog was so violent that no-one dared go into the yard. But George could literally take meat out of his mouth. You had to respect that.

Each afternoon after school and at the weekends, Laurie and his brother worked in the café. He was good at school-work, especially at maths. He was good at music too and began learning the piano. He loved Beethoven, and he also loved guns.

He saved his money and bought a set of encyclopedias, which were his pride and joy. He left the encyclopedias in the living room, ignoring his father's requests to put them away, out of sight. In a fit of rage George flung the encyclopedias on to the floor. Laurie was deeply shocked when he saw them strewn, broken backed, over the floor. This act was unforgivable. He would never forget the sight of those books, spread-eagled on the floor, and the power of his father's arm that could sweep them there.

He passed the Intermediate Certificate in 1953 and went to Moree to work as a jackeroo. He loved work on the land. He worked there for a year, when an old farm hand, who'd taught him a thing or two about cards, persuaded him that it was no life unless you had land of your own. And for that you needed money. He sold Laurie a gun for £10 and Laurie returned to the city where he got a job as a storeman and made good money playing cards on the side.

Two months later he entered into an adventure with an older boy, Jimmy, and two of Jimmy's friends. Jimmy knew a man who had a gun and the plan was to hold him up with Laurie's gun and demand he hand it over. Laurie met up with two of Jimmy's friends, and three foolish young people, with Jimmy keeping watch down at the corner, went to the wrong house, 29 instead of 39, and held up the wrong man. This man didn't have a gun, so they took his money, £10.70, and two packets of cigarettes. They pulled the cord from the phone, tied the man to the gas stove, and told him "Don't tell the police about this, or we'll come back and do you over." They divided the money with Jimmy and headed for home.

Next morning the police came to George's shop, suspecting, for reasons never revealed, that it was Laurie who had been involved. Laurie still had the gun in his bag, and although it was his first offence, he was charged with armed robbery. He was 16 years old.

Bail was requested on the undertaking that he obey his parents and the doctor, and that he be considered for treatment at Broughton Hall, a mental asylum for children. The magistrate believed, on the basis of the facts presented to him, that in-patient treatment was necessary. Laurie was committed to Broughton Hall where he was diagnosed with schizophrenia. For the next 8 months he was subjected several times each week to insulin coma therapy.

This treatment, also known as insulin shock therapy, was extremely unpleasant and dangerous. Insulin injections first thing in the morning led to two or three hours of low blood sugar levels during which the patient successively became confused, weak, could not walk properly and had slurred speech; there were two kinds of coma, a wet and a dry, and occasionally a grand mal seizure which was regarded as desirable. To end the coma, glucose was administered through a gavage tube, inserted through the nasal passage and into the stomach. On waking the patient had slow responses with slurred speech. Within 15 minutes they could recognise the nurses, and if they'd had a wet coma, they found themselves drenched from sweat and saliva, and often soiled. The mortality rate varied from 1% to 10% of patients treated. Prolonged coma in which the patient did not respond to glucose was a constant threat. Three months was the recommended maximum period for this treatment.

During the 8 months of Laurie's treatment, the magistrate was tenacious, calling repeatedly for Laurie to appear in court, suggesting that the treatment was a way to avoid sentencing. The lawyer and psychologist resisted, saying he was not well enough to appear, and that there was no way he would be held in a public institution on false pretences. When the asylum began allowing weekend release, the magistrate would wait no longer to have the matter settled. Laurie was committed to five years hard labour on a prison farm.

In prison he was studious and cooperative and after two years he was released. He went back home and enrolled at a Technical College to complete his Leaving Certificate.

Sydney in the late 50s was a violent city run by gangsters and corrupt police. The police organised armed holdups, framed criminals, and made a great deal of money from bribery payments from people involved in running illegal gambling, prostitution and abortion rackets. Police verballing and manipulation of evidence were standard practice.

Only weeks before his final exam Laurie found someone who would sell him a pistol, a Luger 9mm, which he kept hidden in a tin in the pianola, just near the bellows. He dressed up in a fine suit and hat, and took his pistol with him to the central business district of the city. Walking randomly into an office, he checked it out first, then returned with white handkerchief tied to cover his face. He held up the receptionist at the front desk and demanded money. She gave him £5 from her handbag. He was fascinated by the detailed report in the newspaper next day, though annoyed that the witness got the detail wrong. She said it was a blue scarf, but it was definitely a white handkerchief.

Laurie gave up thoughts of his exam. He repeated his routine of hold-ups twice more. In one he got £4.10, but in the other there were two women who began screaming. He smacked each one on the cheek hard, to quiet them, but they had no money, so he left. When the police visited George, he told them about the pistol in the pianola. The hold-ups were for kicks, Laurie explained later, to the police, not the money. But at home, he kept his room locked and bolted, wearing several keys tied with a shoelace to his belt. Inside his room was a collection of weapons and disguises and maps. He admitted to the police when they inspected his room and its contents that he was making plans for holding up a bank. Once more, he found himself in court, where the psychologist likened him to Darcy Dugan, a notorious armed robber at large in Australia at that time, saying he believed he would not hesitate to fire his pistol, as Dugan had done. Laurie swore never to trust another psychologist from that day on.

Again he was sentenced to five years hard labour, even though none of the witnesses could identify him in a line-up.

There were two warders in the prison, "screws," that he came to hate with a deep and enduring hatred. He decided if he ever knew he was going to die he would take them with him.

He got prison tattoos to show he was tough, one of which said "I love mother." He gave up smoking when he realized the rations of cigarettes were a means of manipulating and controlling prisoners. He used his ration as a currency that bought him things he needed. He learned to sense people coming up behind him and to knock them down before they could touch him. He learned to defend himself with a razor blade embedded in cork, and by becoming handy with his fists. A fist became a bunch-of-fives. His name changed to Larry.

Again he was studious. He got a job in the prison library, and completed his Leaving Certificate with impressive results gaining the nickname "professor." He was obsessive about cleanliness, keeping his cell spotless, flushing the toilet as soon as he defecated so the smell of shit would not get into his clothes while he wiped himself and pulled up his pants. He looked forward each Sunday to the weekend newspaper and cut out the half page Prince Valiant strip, accumulating the long story week by week. He kept a note-book of complex mathematical ideas he was working through. He became a model prison-er, studying long hours in his cold cell, wrapped in a blanket.

In the early sixties the gaol system was looking for new and innovative rehabilitation strategies. They encouraged him to enrol in a university degree by external studies in a rural university. For each four-day residential school, he would be accompanied by a warder. He scored high distinctions in all his work. After two years of this experiment, he was allowed to go alone to the university and trusted to bring himself back.

For the first time he was free to develop a sexual relationship.

Finding very soon that one of the young women he had slept with was pregnant, a train of events unfolded that had its own momentum. A deal was struck. He would be released from gaol, he would marry, he would work as a computer programmer at the rural university where he was studying, and he would complete his degree with honours. He would not go back to Sydney, and instead he would create a normal life for himself. He accepted the plan, though not before surreptitiously checking the back of the neck of the young woman to see if it was clean under her long hair, and checking that she had good child-bearing hips. George had always told him he must do both of those things before taking a wife. He told her nothing of the experience at Broughton Hall. She was twenty and had a degree in Psychology and English. She persuaded her parents to give her permission to marry, the only other options at that time being illegal abortion or putting the baby up for adoption. She believed she had little to offer the world herself, except a capacity to love, whereas he was a mathematical genius, and had suffered a great deal. She could devote her own life to making a good life possible for him.

Laurie was appalled, once they were married, by the demands she made on him. In the first days together, she said, after embracing him as they passed each other in the hallway, that she hoped they would never take each other for granted, or fail to notice each other. He said he couldn't wait until they did. If she embraced him, he read it as a demand for sex. Once she told him, afterwards, she had just wanted to be affectionate, and he laughed loudly. He hoped she would soon learn not to be affectionate.

Soon after the marriage she enrolled in a summer sculpture school. She met him for lunch, excited at what she was learning. But when she told him the teacher had shown her how she could change her clay sculpture to make it more interesting, a suggestion she was not really sure she accepted, he found himself deeply outraged at any other man speaking to his wife, let alone telling her what to do. She argued, but finally gave up the school. He felt safer after that.

When her friends visited, he tried at first, to be welcoming, but after only one visit he found himself so stressed by their presence in his space that he asked her to write to all her friends telling them not to visit.

When the baby was born, the first thing she did when she arrived home from hospital was to offer him the baby. She expected him to hold him, he knew, but he couldn't.

He insisted that she close her bank account and place her savings in his own account. Then each week he withheld part of her meagre weekly shopping allowance, saying she should learn to make do with less. He ruled that she could have one new dress each year, and one pair of shoes. She knitted and sewed all of her clothes, and his, and the children's. Once, when the weekly allowance was not enough to last to the end of the week, and she had only Greek fried zucchinis to give him for lunch, he threw the plate and food against the wall and stalked out, going to the shop to buy food for himself.

They moved to an old derelict house where the rent was lower. Here he became obsessed with the idea that she might be seeing her friends secretly. When, on his way to work, he saw the car of one of them parked nearby, he became certain that she was having an affair. He hid outside the house instead of going to work to see if he could catch them, and for two weeks on end waited and watched. During all of that time he could not talk to her or explain what was going on. When finally she broke open his silence by shouting at him, he beat her unconscious. He thought it was over then, but when she came to, she reassured him, telling him she still loved him.

When her parents, who lived in another town, dropped by unexpectedly on their way to a holiday resort, she explained, as he had instructed her to, that her ink-black eyes were due to bumping into a cupboard door. But his father-in-law suggested Larry go with him for a beer, and there in the pub, man-to-man, explained that men of character did not beat their wives. He understood, he said, that women were frustrating, and that it was tempting to hit them if they were frigid, as his own wife was, and as he presumed his daughter was. But men of character learn to desist, he explained, no matter the provocation.

He was in no doubt that poor Larry had been provoked.

He grew more paranoid, as time passed. And if she challenged him over even a minor decision, his rage overcame him. Once in an argument over whether she could spend 60 cents on a garden sprinkler, in order to ensure she could keep the garden alive after the second baby was born, he rammed his head against the wall and fell foaming at the mouth to the floor. She helped him up and soothed him then comforted the baby who had seen it all.

One day when she told him that the rooster had tried to attack her when she was gathering the eggs, he went out in the dark and began to strangle the rooster, stopping only seconds before it died. Soon after, he came home from work and as soon as he walked in the door he knew she had done something wrong. She looked terrified. He made her tell him. She had gone to the doctor and spilled her guts, and the doctor had said she needed help—he would ring her parents. In a rage, he forced her to go straight down to the public phone box and ring her parents to tell them it was a false alarm. Tell them nothing is wrong.

Next day her mother arrived to take her home to speak to her father. It was his turn to be terrified. He'd be back in gaol before he knew it. But to his amazement, she told him, when she arrived home next day, that his father-in-law was on his side. He'd asked how often they had sex, and decided that that was the problem. Predictable. The horny old bastard is obsessed with sex. Told her if he were her husband he'd cut her throat if they only had sex once a week. Ordered her to come back and behave like a proper wife, to be sexual, to "play him like a violin"! Jesus! He felt as if his guts were being ripped out.

They moved again, on her father's advice, this time buying a cottage with a substantial back yard in which he could grow vegetables. The vegetable garden took up half the garden. Processing all the vegetables for the freezer would keep her busy. They bought butchering knives and a cleaver, in order to cut up their own meat, and so live more cheaply. He put the butchering implements in a locked trunk and told her to hide the key, explaining that he couldn't be trusted not to use them in the wrong way. Still, after being out of gaol for some years, if she accidentally walked up behind him, without letting him know she was coming, he would knock her to the ground. He couldn't extinguish that reflex action. She had learned to call out to warn him, but out in the new garden the wind could carry away her voice.

One day he decided to teach her to play chess. His method of teaching was to show her she had made a wrong move by taking her piece. When, in her upper-middle class way she exclaimed, after several such moves, "oh you bugger," his brain fused, and a flashing white light blinded him. The board and the pieces flew up into the air, hitting the ceiling with a loud crack. He stood in the middle of the room, trembling, fists clenched, hunched over. He could not possibly tell her what her words had done to him.

Once they went out to a dinner dance organised at his work-place. A gambling room had been set up adjacent to the dining room and he looked forward to trying out his old skills. He had no trouble winning, but was constantly distracted, worrying about who his wife might be talking to. He continually left the gaming room to watch what she was doing. It was unbearable to see her pleasure in talking to the people at their table. They left early and he resolved that would be the last such outing.

Every day he insisted that the house be cleaned from top to bottom, so there was no dirt anywhere. Even so, one night, when she walked in bare feet from the shower to the bed, he kicked her hard so she fell out of the bed on to the floor. He told her she was filthy walking on the floor without slippers.

When the second baby was due, he smacked the child, not yet turned two, for quietly whimpering when he got up in the dark to take himself through the dark house to the toilet. Didn't they know to be silent when he was there? She was so angry with him, telling him how the baby had learned, just today, to take himself to the toilet with his eyes shut, so he could do it at night to save his mummy having two babies in nappies at the same time. She was so upset with him that her waters broke and the new baby was born two hours later.

He worked long hours at his studies. The babies must never cry at night and disturb his study or his sleep. He insisted that she not turn the heater on at night when she got up to feed the new baby, born at the beginning of winter. Yes, it was icy cold but they should learn to be strong as he had had to learn to be. He shouted at the two year old if he left a painting on the end of his daddy's desk, hoping he would like the beautiful gift he had made for him while he was at work. "Who left this on my desk? Get it off!"

The two year old began to stutter, and his beautiful paintings turned to black, every day, pages and pages filled with black paint. That made Larry scared and he agreed with his wife to be less hard on the child.

A third child was born 15 months after the second. Larry insisted the children learn to walk without holding onto the furniture, for fear they might dirty it. He smacked the oldest child if he made any noise when he walked on the wooden floor in the hallway, so disturbing his studies, or if he left any of his small toys in the long grass.

She came home from the hospital with the third baby, two days after he was born. Janet had come to help out, but he'd insisted she come before the baby was due in case he was born while the exam was on. As soon as the wife came home it was time for Janet to go back to George.

She couldn't sleep because when she shut her eyes she felt like she was falling down a bottomless chasm, and that all she consisted of was a thin scream falling and falling. He called the doctor, who gave her sleeping pills. When the doctor left he confiscated the pills. Otherwise she might sleep leaving the babies to cry, and disturb his study or his sleep.

Each day he left the house at exactly the same time, carrying the lunch his wife had packed for him, having eaten the porridge she cooked for him and drunk the freshly squeezed orange juice. The babies had not made any noise or disturbed him before he left. It was all under control. Sometimes he would come home unexpectedly to check on her, to make sure no-one was there. He couldn't bear to see her idle, or playing with the children in the garden. He must find more tasks to keep her busy.

He borrowed money from his father-in-law to buy a car, though he couldn't drive. He insisted she teach him, and that the children sit in the back while she did so. She was opposed to this plan, pointing out that it was dangerous, but he was adamant. She drove the car out onto a deserted back lane and handed over the steering wheel to him. He did not follow her instructions, and fairly quickly threw the car into a skid. She yelled at him to stop, and to get out, which he did, and she drove them home in a rage. He could see he had been wrong, and felt shamed. He agreed to pay for lessons.

He rarely talked to people at work. But one day he heard about a fancy new restaurant that had opened up. It was their wedding anniversary, which they had never celebrated. It seemed a good idea to go out. The table-service was slow and his rage grew as they waited. Eventually they ordered a steak that was to be cooked on a new-fangled hot plate brought to the table. The hot plate took a long time to come, and then when it did, it was stone cold, and the waiter didn't know how to heat it. It was a farcical night, but there was no laughter, no chance of any conversation, since both of them were focussed on containing the volcanic rage that threatened to burst from him at any moment. They didn't try to go out again.

Time passed. Then one, morning instead of having his breakfast on the table on time, he found her standing in the kitchen with her hand locked onto the orange she was squeezing, unable to move, or to speak. He couldn't get her to move or to hear him. He got the banana chair and put it up in the living room, picked her rigid body up and lay her down on the banana chair, placing each of the three children on the floor near her, where she could see them. He left for work without any breakfast.

Some weeks later she got this thing about not being able to eat, said she couldn't swallow. He called the doctor who said to give her grated carrot and grated apple and left a prescription for anti-depressants. He picked a carrot from the garden and grated it, but still she couldn't eat. He yelled at her that she was trying to get at him. She would put the grated food in her mouth and chew, but end up dropping it out of her mouth saying her throat refused to swallow it. When she got the depression pills, he confiscated them. No wife of his was going on anti-depressants. He told her she could only have one if she was really desperate. The truth was, she was weak and letting him down just when the exams were coming up. He figured he needed to find a woman with guts who was strong enough. This one was no good to him. He began to visit a couple of women in town, who ran their own businesses, but they gave him the cold shoulder. They were weak too. Gutless.

Then disaster struck. She was approached by the Headmistress of a private girls' school and offered a part-time job. There was a state-wide shortage of teachers. She accepted the job, although he forbade it. She said she was going mad and had to get out in order to be able to keep going. He would not let her use the car to drive to work, and he threatened the baby-sitters until they quit in fear. He rang the headmistress and told her his wife had said terrible things about her. But still she managed to keep her job. On one rare occasion when he did let her drive the car to work, he inspected it with a torch when he got home

to make sure it was not damaged. He found a scratch and came inside holding aloft a tiny thorn from the bush beside the driveway, that had green paint
on it, claiming that the thorn proved it was she who had made the scratch on
the car. She told him he was mad and that she wasn't going to listen to him. She
wouldn't even look at the paint on the thorn.

The only solution was to go to another place and start again. He fantasized
about going to the south pole, away from people. Then there would be no
school for her to teach at. He would need another job. First he would need the
authorities to remove his name from the prison files. He wrote to them asking
for this to happen. He would need to look more presentable. He'd lost some
teeth while in prison, and decided to get false teeth so it would not be so visible to any future employer that he was an ex-con. He had all his top teeth pulled
out in one day. He forbade her to speak to anyone.

He got a letter from the prison authorities saying he could not have his
name removed from the files, advising him that he would have to tell the
truth of his past to any future employer. The exam results came out at the same
time, and he'd only come second, beaten by a woman. He could not believe it
was possible to be beaten by a woman. True, she was clever, and true she had
been nice to him, but she should not have got first place.

His wife wrote to his mother telling her about his violence toward her and
the children. She wrote back saying she was really sorry things had become so
bad. He found the letter, and was filled with bitter rage. His mother had
betrayed him.

His wife told him he needed help. She said that clearly she could not do
for him whatever it was he needed. So she was going to betray him too? He told
her he wouldn't support her if she left. He forbade her to ring her father, but
she did. At least he stuck by him, telling his daughter "it's obvious poor Larry
has hit a brick wall again" telling her that the violence was her own fault. Her
father told her that she would not get custody if she left the marriage, and he
told his own wife that if she helped their daughter in any way to escape she
could leave home.

He had begun to have repeated images of killing himself, and of killing the
two screws in Goulburn. They deserved to die. He told her he hadn't yet
decided if he would kill her and the children. She told him he needed to see a
psychologist, but he refused point blank. It was she who was crazy, not him.
One afternoon when he walked in the door, unexpectedly early, before she had
the kids ready for the regime of silence, she told him that it was like black death
when he walked in the door.

Then one Friday his wife and children were not there when he got home.
There was a note saying they would be back on Sunday. He was so shaken, that
when he took out his new teeth to clean them, he dropped them on the tiled

floor and they broke. As he picked them up from the bathroom floor, he felt all his life energy leak out of him. He was like a zombie, a walking dead man. He spent the weekend in limbo, drawing plans for a cross bow, and a nymph who was beckoning him to his death.

When she got back on Sunday she told him that she would stay. The minister of her sister's fundamentalist church had told her she could only leave if her husband ordered her to leave. He had even said that if he killed them it would be God's will.

But for him it was too late. He had no life left in him.

Her brother came to stay, which outraged him, but he had no energy left to make her do what he wanted. He got his teeth mended, and for a few days managed to follow his routines, to go to work, to water the garden. Then one morning when she was trying to light the fire in the stove, she couldn't open the back door to take the tray of ash out. The lock was stuck. She headed for the front door. He grabbed hold of her, telling her he would show her how to open it. He did not want her walking with the ash out the front door. She wrenched herself out of his grasp and went out the front door. He followed her back into the kitchen where she was struggling to get the stove alight. The flue was blocked. She wasn't going to get his breakfast on to the table on time. He told her she was getting at him. She pointed out that if he refused to let men into the house to clean the flue, which had been blocked now for weeks, she couldn't get the fire lit and cook his breakfast on time. She was talking back and he couldn't stand it. He grabbed her by the throat and squeezed hard to stop her voice, to stop her breath. He wanted her dead; but suddenly he looked behind him, as if there might be someone there watching. No-one. He dumped her onto the bench by the stove. He began to search for the place where she had hidden the key to the chest with the knives and cleaver. Couldn't find them. Went down to the shed to get a bicycle tube, packed some underwear into his briefcase, and walked to the front door. She was standing in the kitchen, holding onto the bench. "So it's like black death when I walk in the door is it. You'll never see me again."

He went out to the car and started it up. Into town to the insurance office to cancel his life insurance policy. To the bank to close his account. To the garage to fill the car with petrol. To the Post Office to post his father his gold watch and the money. Owe the old bastard nothing. The wife must have nothing. Down the long road to Sydney to stay overnight with his aunt. To whom he told nothing. Washed out his shirt so it didn't stink of sweat. To Goulburn to find the two screws. Nowhere to be found. Energy dangerously low. Put the letter from his mother in his pocket. She'd be sorry when they found that on him. Out onto a lonely country road to eat the sleeping pills he'd confiscated. Fix the bicycle tube to the exhaust. And so to sleep at last, alone.

From Jonathan 7–4-10

I have sat for many days with Bronwyn's writing about ethics and the story of Larry that follows.

I have been on a break from work over the Easter period, with the time that this has given to allow her writing to find its way. Earlier this morning, a Tuesday, I read this chapter again over coffee as a woman at a table opposite conducted an argument over the phone with someone I took to be her partner. The issue between them involved the partner having landed her with a bill she had no choice but to pay, about which she was angry. "I have no choice, do I?" she kept saying. "I have no choice, no choice," her voice rising to become loud enough to distract a number of us sitting near her. I could not work out the full story but the pain and anger I read into her responses both intruded upon my time with Bronwyn's writing and echoed something of the story I was reading.

In Bronwyn's note attached to the draft of this chapter, she spoke of being on edge, wondering what response it would bring. Standing with her now as, in a sense, I take her story and find a way to give it back to her, I am on an edge too. I wonder how it will be possible to respond. I feel awed but honoured.

This is a chapter about ethics and the story of Larry comes as a challenge. It is as if it asks of me: how will you meet me? Will you encounter me as, in Bergson's terms, "descent," as a lesson in how to live or not to live, or as "ascent," open to how it might create? Can you—Jonathan—experience this story and allow it to take you into the Deluzian not-yet-known? Or will you bring to it only those codes and practices that govern what is regarded as "good" and "evil"? Are you able to work within yourself, in Bronwyn's words, "in the spaces opened up in relation to other aspects or experiences of Being" or will you impose your concepts of an essence against which you will find the protagonists wanting? Might it be possible for you to do world-making here?

So, I find myself with this story wanting to allow myself to be open. I seek to respond with "practices of acknowledgement" (White, 2000), rather than those of applause or condemnation, to some of those moments that affect me as I read:

"When the father did not get his way, his rage was spectacular. Sometimes grabbing the lintel of the doorway above him he smashed his head, repeatedly, against it."

I observe this scene, my heart torn. This is the way that I create it from Bronwyn's words:

Laurie (as he was then), still a small boy, watches as his father does violence to himself. In the first home in which he lived Laurie spent hours alone with his brother in the dark room, his mother taken from him by his father's demands—though probably Laurie did not understand this dynamic at the time. He may only have known the experience of being abandoned. At the time of these two lines, he is now living in the country. Left on their own still, given their father's expectations of his mother that she devote herself to working the farm, he and his brother's play is, it appears, regularly disturbed by the sound of hitting, like wood on wood. On the occasion that I am witnessing it here, they rush to find its source, though they have heard it before and know what it will be. Laurie sees his father's head beating the door frame. Laurie can see the marks on his father's head gradually turn to blood and bruise. He wants to cry out for him to stop but can't. He knows that to do so carries risk. He has learnt that. He doesn't want to be hurt. So he and his brother stand, out of sight, until the hitting stops and they then retreat. Their mother is on the floor, weeping silently, holding onto and hiding behind a chair. They walk slowly back outside and resume their game.

"Each afternoon after school and at the weekends, Laurie and his brother worked in the café. He was good at school-work, especially maths. He was good at music too and began learning the piano. He loved Beethoven and he also loved guns."

I am shocked by the juxtaposition of his love of Beethoven and guns. I long to excise those final five words of the final sentence. He loved Beethoven. He could play the piano. He did well at school. But guns gave him something that these interests, achievements and talents didn't.

There was a shooting club at school. I joined when I was eleven. One afternoon each week we would walk to the shooting range in the school grounds. I would lie on the ground alongside a handful of other boys under Colonel Culverhouse's supervision. I would couch the rifle in my left hand with the butt pushed against my right shoulder, right index finger resting on the trigger. I enjoyed the effect of drawing that finger slowly towards me and the jolt as the small bullet sped from the barrel towards the target.

I have a recurring nightmare that I have killed and that only I know. There is a body that I have hidden, or buried, or thrown into a lake, sometime in the past, and I have not been found out. I know, though. I know. I am unable to deny that it was my doing. I have not had this dream for a few years but I am sure that it will come again.

He was committed to "Broughton Hall, a mental asylum for children....He was subjected several times each week to insulin coma therapy."

The violence done to him, to this young man. I have written "oh, oh, oh" in the margin of my text. It is the only word that I can find.

"He would create a normal life for himself. He accepted the plan, though not before surreptitiously checking the back of the neck of the young woman to see if it was clean under her long hair."

Bronwyn is here in the story. She has been here as the narrator, of course, up until now, writing of Laurie's life before she met him. She is introduced to us as the young woman with the long hair whose neck Laurie has to check for cleanliness. Later in this paragraph, Bronwyn writes of herself that she "believed she had little to offer the world...except a capacity to love."

The Bronwyn that I see wears her hair short. The experience of the Bronwyn that I encounter is of a resolute, clear-thinking, strong woman. Her capacity to love endures. From the Laurie/Larry that I have come to know through Bronwyn, and through the insight she gives of the light that she saw in him, I find myself understanding how she would be hopeful, even though as a reader I know the future for them. I read on from this point and become aware of how much she had to deal with and of the strength she needed to find a way through.

The writing in this chapter is Bronwyn's story as well as Larry's. Is this one way of understanding how Bronwyn is, as she writes of being co-implicated in his story?

These lines bring back to me the experience, maybe three years ago, of counselling a woman in her 60s whose husband had died some six years previously. I have not thought about her for a long time. She was haunted by her husband, having been married to him since her late teens, and during those thirty years she had been relentlessly put down, criticised, insulted and more. During their life together she remained hopeful, despite everything, that she would one day do enough to please him. She told me, six years since his death, that she couldn't bear the guilt that she felt for feeling relieved that he had gone. We met for a number of months. As we were finishing she was struggling to resist pressure from her son, who was himself badly treated by his father, to help with his embryonic business. He lived in the north of the country and phoned her most days to check on what she had done and to berate her for what she had failed to achieve on his behalf. As we talked she began to realise that this pressure on her had resonances of how her husband had treated her. We arranged to meet one more time but she did not attend her appointment. I have not heard from her since.

"Once in an argument over whether she could spend 60 cents on a garden sprinkler..., he rammed his head against the wall and fell foaming at the mouth to the floor. She helped him up and soothed him then comforted the baby who had seen it all."

Standing to one side of this scene, I look from one to the other: at the man who has become his father in the inflicting of such damage upon himself; and at the woman who has to choose whose pain to attend to first, her damaged husband or her distressed baby. Though unstated, her own pain is palpable.

"He shouted at the two year old if he left a painting on the end of his daddy's desk, hoping he would like the beautiful gift he had made for him while he was at work."

The two-year-old's optimism, his reaching out to his father, like Florence's to her father in Dickens' *Dombey and Son,* is excruciating to witness. Florence can never find in her father the love that she longs for.

I sense that Bronwyn's hope is present here too as she watches her little boy place the painting for Larry, imagining that maybe, just maybe, her baby's gift will find its way to Larry.

Their third child. Her hand and throat locking. Her job. Her telling Larry she could no longer stay. His broken teeth. Her talking back. His leaving with the car. The bank, the garage, Goulbourn. The country road.

"And so to sleep at last, alone."

It is finally over and there is release. This sad, lonely end. I find I want to hold him as he goes, if he will allow me. I doubt he will.

I turn to Bronwyn and her boys and ask if I might sit with them awhile.

From Bronwyn 12–04–10 St Ives

I am deeply moved by what Jonathan has written. I am so comforted by his desire to sit with us, me and my sons, for a while, and by the care he can imagine extending toward Larry at the point of his death. These two imagined moments of "holding" brought me to tears when I read them, and bring tears to my eyes again, each time I think about them. I find a space of longing in myself for that peaceful sitting awhile with my children.

At the time of his death I did not grieve for him. The children and I did not grieve for him. We were thankful to be released from a life we could barely manage, and instantly propelled into a fresh set of problems that began to emerge in the 70s directly out of the unresolved problems of the 60s. I was faced with earning a living in a system that could not see women as legitimate scholars, with establishing women's right to have crèches to care for their children, with studying for higher degrees in an education system that was all about privileged white men, with confronting, again and again, the prejudice against single mothers, with confronting sexual harassment and naming rape within marriage; and for the children, they were faced with living with a history that was, for them, impossible to talk about and best not remembered—not to mention living with a single mother who was always busy and often stressed. We were catapulted chaotically into the freedom that Larry's death granted us.

But his death has stayed with us, invisibly present. It was a heavy price for life.

That he still appeared in my dreams, so many years later, as a monster, was disturbing. I want to be able to greet him with Deleuze's question—how is it to be like this: "How must it be in order to say that? Which manner of Being does this imply?" I wanted to seek "the enveloped modes of existence, and not the transcendent values" (Deleuze, 1980). I don't want to judge him and condemn him any more than I want to judge and condemn myself. We are, like all living beings caught up in, co-implicated in Being, in an emergent life where none is entirely separate from the other.

The way I experience my life can't be disentangled from my marriage or Larry's death. And his death can't be disentangled from his marriage to me. We were in a sense each other's problem, where a "problem is life's way of responding to or questioning what is not itself" (Colebrook, 2002: 21). Just as a tree meets the problem of the large rock underneath it by growing roots around it, so my life is grown around the large immovable rock of an impossible, fatal task that was set for me and that I willingly took up. We were co-implicated in the storyline that said if only I could love well enough, he could heal. The problem I took on was to love well enough. I wrapped my life around it, and the lives of my children, for five terrible years...

Larry's release into the world, and into my care, can be construed as an act of what Nancy (2007b) calls globe-making—firmly embedded in contemporary ethics, and producing over-regulated practices focussed on the production of generic, predictable individuals, responsive to the forces of government, or in Foucault's words, forging docile bodies, bodies "that may be subjected, used, transformed and improved" (Foucault 1977: 136). The progressive 60s did not understand itself that way, of course. The prison authorities who supervised his release understood themselves as doing something unusual, granting freedom where freedom had not usually been granted. It was an experiment in reform, and in some ways it worked. The wild boy who had gone with a gun to rob the wrong person, and who had later configured himself as a masked bandit, knuckled down, earned a living, gave up crime, grew a vegetable garden, studied, paid the bills. But he could not get past a deep paranoia that the prison system, the mental health system, and his life from the beginning, had helped to generate. It was in the cells of his body; his roots had grown out of and around that paranoia.

We all bought into the reform project; and we brought to that project a romantic liberal humanism that suggested that the right kinds of effort would enable us to accomplish the task; and through that effort his (essential) gifts, his genius, would be released for the betterment of society. So apparently simple. *All you need is love.* (After his death I couldn't listen to the clichés of popular music. I still can't. They made me then, and still make me, feel sick). For his part, what he needed to do was work hard. And he did that—his desk took up a whole wall of the living room, and he was rarely absent from it. Like Mrs Ramsay and her 8 children in *To the Lighthouse* (Woolf, 1992), the children and I tiptoed around his irascible dedication to his work.

I had been complicit in the romantic storyline and the disaster that followed.

Integral to its impossibility was that it began with the assumption that I was no-one and he was someone. It was a common story. Every novel I'd ever read was organised around it, and everything my mother had told me was directed toward it. Men were difficult and women must have the strength and resilience to give life to them, while not, in Mrs Ramsay's words, being good enough to tie their shoe strings (Woolf, 1992: 38). The problems I confronted in my marriage were not survivable ones. For either of us. Or for the children.

To say I was co-implicated is not the same as saying I'm guilty, though if one wants to engage in moralistic judgements, as contemporary ethics invites us to do, it is easy enough to invoke guilt by constructing him as vulnerable and me as strong. From a Deleuzian ethics, though, I understand him and me, both, to have been caught up together in trying to solve an unsolvable problem. I see the prison authorities in the 60s as engaging in what seemed at the time like a line of flight, but it was to do with finding a way to ensure his embeddedness in the striations of domesticity and work. Just as I thought that marrying someone so different from the rural middle-class that I grew up in was a line of escape, of flight, from the boredom and striations of that world— only to find myself as thoroughly caught as anyone I've ever met in the striations of marriage, very like Friedan documents them in *The Feminine Mystique* (*Freidan, 1963*).

So why bring this story into our book, into the space of Deleuzian ethics? First, because I was troubled at my monstering of him in my dreams and then by the silence in our writing that followed. It seemed to me that the space in between us, where "us" includes Deleuze, could be one that was able to accommodate him without categorising and judging, where I might safely tell his story in such a way that he could be greeted as Jonathan has greeted him. But also, perhaps, because I thought that we needed to extend what we were doing here, to see how robust our thinking/being was under strain. There is a danger for those of us who've grown up with liberal humanism to romanticise what we do, to present it all as a heroic or romantic journey with no dangers along the way. Lines of flight make creative evolution possible, but they are also dangerous, and they may be destructive. We can, in the hope of safety, stay with Bergson's line of descent, or we can take risks and seek out the line of ascent, of movement toward a future not-yet-known.

Collaborative Writing with Deleuze (B)

In which Bronwyn thinks about how to characterise what JKSB have thought about and practiced in their engagement with Deleuze and collaborative writing.

Collaborative writing is
to listen with all one's ears   with all one's senses
letting listening overtake you
to become no longer an "I" who listens to "you"
but coming into Being through your words

Collaborative writing is
Dangerous   I am vulnerable to your words
to your listening   listening
makes me tremble   stop still in my tracks
gaze off into the distance   lost

Collaborative writing is
To carry the words of the other tenderly
in one's shoulder bag   to spill coffee
To long for the presence of the other
To long to write to the other   and silence

Collaborative writing is
To see again   differently   it is to peel off
the taken-for-granted
to enter a space that is familiar
and bring it vividly to life

Collaborative writing is
shivering on the sand
contemplating the shape of the mountain
wrapped up in a swag in the desert
being and knowing   stuttering   and and and

Collaborative writing is
to be co-implicated with the other
to be present
to be assailed by thoughts   by being...
to be singular   to exist in the space of writing with

I want to ask now, standing on this last of our plateaus, what does Deleuze's *presence* in our collaborative writing demand of us and open up for us? Colebrook's take on his presence was:

> Deleuze took nothing for granted and insisted that the power of life—all life and not just human life—was its power to develop problems. Life poses problems—not just to thinking beings, but to all life....The questions of philosophy, art and science are extensions of *the questioning power of life*, a power that is also expressed in smaller organisms and their tendency to evolve, mutate and *become* (2002: 1)....[Y]ou have to begin by seeing the *problem* of Deleuze's work: whether we can think difference and becoming without relying on common sense notions of identity, reason, the human subject or even "being" (2002: 4). [In *Anti-Oedipus* (Deleuze and Guattari, 2004a)] Deleuze and Guattari argued that life was an open and creative whole of proliferating connections. They celebrate the "schizo" against paranoid "man." Their "schizo" is not a psychological type (not a schizophrenic), but a way of thinking a life not governed by any fixed norm or image of self—a self in flux and becoming, rather than a self that has submitted to law. The schizo is a challenge to the way we think and write....[T]hey argued that schizoanalysis would create new connections, open experience up to new beginnings, and allow us to think differently (2002: 5–6).

Badiou, too, reflects on Deleuze's presence, having had an extended correspondence with him not long before he died, but never having met him face to face. His emphases are different from Colebrook's, and suggest that Deleuze is someone that could never be pinned down with words, but exists in multiple imaginings of him:

> There is an image of Deleuze as, at once, radical and temperate, solitary and convivial, vitalist and democratic. It is fairly commonly believed that his doctrine promotes the heterogeneous multiplicity of desires and encourages their unrestrained realization, that is concerned with the respect and affirmation of differences, and that it thus constitutes a conceptual critique of totalitarianisms, as is indicated, in practice, by the fact that Deleuze kept his distance—in a way that not even Foucault did—from all Stalinist and Maoist involvements. It is believed that he preserved the rights of the body against all terrorizing formalisms; that he made no concession to the spirit of system, but rather constantly commended the Open and movement, advocating an experimentation without preestablished norms. In his method of thinking, which admits only cases and singularities, he is believed to have stood fast against the crushing abstractions of the dialectic. It is equally believed that he participates in modern (postmodern?) "deconstruction," insofar as he carries out a decisive critique of representation, substitutes the logic of sense for the search for the truth, and combats transcendent idealities in the name of the creative immanence of life: in sum, he adds his contribution to the ruin of metaphysics, to the "overturning of Platonism," by promoting, against the sedentary *nomos* of Essences, the nomad *nomos* of precarious actualizations, divergent series, and unpredictable creations....(Badiou, 2000: 9)

Having Deleuze among us has meant that we have refrained from saying what collaborative writing *is* or how it *should* be done. We have not provided a pre-existing formula that might be followed or a template against which good collaborative writing might be judged. Rather we have let collaborative writing evolve, and as we encountered problems, found ways to work with and around those problems. As Colebrook observes: "A problem is a way of creating a future. When plants grow and evolve they do so by way of problems, developing features to avoid predators, to maximise light or to retain moisture....A problem is life's way of responding to or questioning what is not itself" (2002: 21). By keeping our separate voices we have made some of the problems we pose for each other visible; we have kept difference alive in the text, and resisted the move to set up a normative structure for collaborative writing that we might have labelled Deleuzian. We have sought, in the spaces among us, to give expression to our multiple singularities, those differences that might otherwise go unnoticed or be subsumed into a structure or an essence or a set of normativities. The problems we have encountered in our writing to each other have not been "resolved," but worked with to enable us to arrive at a new point of understanding. Sometimes problems arose that were beyond us, and they have, to some extent, disappeared from this text, though they are still there in the silences and absences.

In keeping our separate voices we have not sought to solidify ourselves into subjects or subjectivities, but the reverse, to open ourselves to the endless possibilities of becoming—becoming other to what we were, becoming what we might be in this space. As Bergson writes: "I change, then, without ceasing. But this is not saying enough. Change is far more radical than we are at first inclined to suppose....[This is not movement from one state to another but] the state itself is nothing but change" (Bergson, 1998: 1–2).

To the extent that we afforded each other a space of attentive listening we created an amorous space, a voluptuous space. For Deleuze (1973: 140), the *concept* of love was as open as possible. Colebrook elaborates this openness when she writes:

> Love is the encounter with another person that opens us up to a possible world. This concept does not take a form of love—the couple—and then say this is what love *is*. The *concept* of love as "a possible encounter with a whole new world" allows us to think of forms of love that are not yet given, that are not actual but virtual. A concept, for Deleuze, is just this power to move beyond what we know and experience to think how experience might be extended. (Colebrook, 2002: 17)

To write collaboratively *with* Deleuze opens up a conceptual space in which we are seized by thought. Rather than imagining ourselves as four separate subjects originating thought about collaborative writing, we open ourselves up to where thinking and doing collaborative writing with Deleuze might take us. Our relation with the outside is not personal; we are no longer the originators of our thoughts; the thoughts are already happening within life that is much bigger than our separate selves. What we have done, is to open ourselves to seeing what happens to ourselves alongside those thoughts, and to seeing where being enveloped in those thoughts might take us, separately and together.

Deleuze is insistent on both the immediate relevance of ourselves as affective, thinking beings, as facets of Being, and at the same time, the giving up of our subjective pretensions. He developed the figure of the automaton precisely to demolish those "subjective pretensions." The automaton constitutes the "outside as agency of active force, takes hold of a body, selects an individual and submits it to the choice of choosing ...Thinking is not the spontaneous effusion of a personal capacity. It is the power, won only with the greatest difficulty *against oneself*, of being constrained to the world's play" (Badiou, 2000: 12). To enter this conceptual space we have had to be willing to go where we are borne by its possibilities; none of us directing it or planning it, but seeing where the act of collaboration with each other, with Deleuze, might take us.

As it happened we travelled a lot during the time we were writing and the spaces in our lives that the travel opened up created both time to write, and fresh and surprising moments of being that we could write into. The flow of words opened up a space between us, among us, that made a particular kind of reflection on those moments of being possible. At the same time, the moments of being did not exist independent of the space they were written into. Deleuze and us found ourselves chosen to write into, create, a space in which collaboration could happen, in which we could come to know and be differently, within that space, not as individuals with separate identities, but more like conjoint quintuplets divided, and writing into the space of each other, joined—not always agreeing with each other, not always hearing each other, but carrying the other with us in our bodies, in our imagination.

Deleuze's emphasis on *and* rather than *or*, required of us that we converge in one stream, and at the same time be open to lines of flight that were divergent, unexpected, breaking open the warm safe folds that made life seem familiar, safe, the same. It also required that we leave our moralisms at the door before we started; we were not here to judge each other against some abstract standard, nor here to insist that we follow some preconceived plan, nor yet were we to abandon affect, our bodily specificities, or the complex challenges that life threw up for each of us. We have monitored the way each of the other's lives have touched us—set hearts beating, set teeth to nail biting, made us safe or not safe, making a living organism of ourselves, together, searching out together the question of what Deleuze means for us, for Being, and for doing what we set out to do.

In case the maintenance of our separate voices might be misread as a narcissistic revelation of our pre-existing selves, it is important to emphasize the anti-humanist impulse of our exploration. Deleuze, like other poststructuralist writers, talks about an *anti-humanism* that moves us beyond the personal narcissism and paranoia that permeates so much of current day thought and action. In advocating that we remain open to becoming not what we are already, he invites us constantly to forget who we are and to open up the evolutionary possibilities of the not-yet-known. By thinking of our experiences as flows and intensities that are aspects of Being, of the One-All, rather than markers of our fragile identities, we are potentially freed of the narcissism and paranoia that go with defending identities. Within humanism the self is imagined against some external ideal and is necessarily always found wanting. In a Deleuzian approach, life is affirmed in its *haecceity*, in being present within moments of being, in movement toward the not-yet-known. Even repetition is not a stale recounting of the already known, but beginning again, within life itself. In freeing oneself of the burden of lying at the centre of an ego-bound existence, this way of thinking frees oneself of oneself; one is released from narcissism and paranoia into a radical relationality, into the spaces in-between, the intensities and flows of Being.

In this way of thinking we are co-extensive with others, co-implicated with others—with human, animal and earth others, and we are no longer forced into a mold that is too tight, too rational, or too moralistic. In Bergson's words:

> ...who can say where individuality begins and ends, whether the living being is one or many, whether it is the cells that associate themselves into the organism or the organism which dissociates itself into cells? In vain we force the living into this or that one of our molds. All the molds crack. They are too narrow, above all too rigid, for what we try to put into them. Our reasoning, so sure of itself among things inert, feels ill at ease on this new ground. It would be difficult to cite a biological discovery due to pure reasoning. And most often, when

experience has finally shown us how life goes to work to obtain a certain
result, we find its way of working is just that of which we should never have
thought. (Bergson, 1998: x)

We have *endured*, in a Bergsonian sense, through this writing. Our
thoughts and memories that we have written about do not pre-exist this
writing, but are emergent within it:

Duration is the continuous progress of the past which gnaws into the future and
swells as it advances. And as the past grows without ceasing, so also there is
no limit to its preservation. Memory, as we have tried to prove, is not a faculty of putting away recollections in a drawer, or of inscribing them in a register. There is no register, no drawer. (Bergson, 1998: 4)

And so...

The collaborative writing that has evolved here has drawn both
from collective biography and from nomadic writing.

From collective biography it draws the practice of beginning with a conceptual problem, and our problem here was: what does it mean in
thought and practice to bring collaborative writing alongside Deleuze?
How can we know and practice what Deleuze does with his concepts?
Deleuzian concepts reach toward the not-yet-said, the not-yet-imagined. They stretch the mind in a virtual movement, in a line of flight, a
creative arc toward the not-yet-known. Our task was to find the way of
doing that, together, knowing and doing it together, through our collaborative writing. We used our own embodied memories and experiences
to breathe life into the exploration. We wrote our way into, and thought
about, moments of being, and we engaged in open listening as this is
practiced in collective biography. We could not spend days together, as
we usually do in collective biography workshops, and so we had to rely
on email to speak to each other, and to listen to each other. Our story-
telling was similar to collective biography in that it generated embodied accounts of moments of being, not relying on clichés and
explanations, but seeking the singular sensations and intensities, drawing on intellect, intuition, the sensori-motor experience of interiors/exte-
riors, selves/others and the infinite resources of language. We sought in
telling and listening not to tell of individual identities closed up on
themselves like eggs, but to open up the flows of Being and of Thought

that did not belong to, or originate from, any one of us alone. We were emergent in the telling; what was important was not the teller but the telling.

The particular quality of listening that we engaged in, that is informed by the practices of collective biography involved paying attention, not just with our minds, but our whole bodies. It involved listening carefully—with care—caring enough to hear what was said; it involved asking, how is it to be *this*, in this moment—coming to know internally. It involved existing fully in the moment of listening, going beyond the binaries of you and me, speaker and listener. It involved listening without judgement, giving up on moralism, giving up on the ego that seeks to defend and criticise and judge. It involved willing vulnerability to the other, an openness to the breakdown of what one knows already, an openness to the knowledge that undoes the already known, an openness to the abjected other that lives at one's borders. This was what we took with us from collective biography.

Our collaborative writing was nomadic in that it documented the flows in-between that are rarely visible in collective biography writing. Each nomadic writer seeks the moments of being, the haecceities, where binaries dissolve. The individual intensities generated in the space-in-between are not stories to be told, listened to, written, read, listened to, re-written, as in collective biography, but footprints in the sand, a trace of footprints of one traveller then another, in which desert, footprints, sandstorms, the intensity of blue in the sky, grains of sand, the black silhouette of the bird, are traces on the page opening new pathways, new possibilities of seeing, of being, of knowing. Each one struggles with their own intensities, their own capacity or incapacity to hear what is said, to read the footprints in the sand, to withstand the storm, to be the storm. They may pass each other on the sand-dunes not knowing the other is there, not registering the path the other is mapping out. The patterns of footsteps criss-cross the desert, now vivid, now erased. The nomad becomes eagle, off on a new line of flight, taking advantage of an unexpected eddy of wind, seeing the criss-crossing paths from above, comprehending the patterns, the connections, the disconnections, the point where something not yet able to be said was traced. The nomad becomes fish, moving with the wave, a swelling of the intense blue sea that washes into the desert and takes advantage of its sagging; it becomes wind, blowing grains of sand making a new smooth place not yet trodden; it becomes a single grain of sand in the eye, becomes tear, becomes drop of blood, becomes heart stilled forever. The nomad knows the desert in the hot soles of its feet, in the hardness of the ridged sand settled into fixed patterns, and in the movement of sand, in its flux. The nomad is that hard sand, and it is the thousand flowers that bloom when it rains. The nomads, together, become their own movements, and in that becoming are co-implicated in each other, in the earth, the sky, the water. This was what we took from nomadic writing.

Collaborative writing with Deleuze is creative and unpredictable. It reaches toward that which cannot yet be said, cannot yet be known. It is precarious and divergent (Badiou, 2000: 9). It is not representation, but invention. It is an immanent plane of composition...

References

Bachelard, G. (1969) *The poetics of space* (trans. Maria Jolas), Boston: Beacon Press.

Badiou, A. (2000) *Deleuze. The clamor of being* (trans. Louise Burchill), Minneapolis: University of Minnesota Press.

Badiou, A. (2002) *Ethics. An essay on the understanding of evil* (trans. Peter Hallward), London: Verso.

Bergson, H. (1998) *Creative evolution* (trans. Arthur Mitchell), Mineola: Dover Publications Inc.

Braidotti, R. (1994) 'Toward a new nomadism: feminist Deleuzian tracks; or, metaphysics and metabolism,' in C. V. Boundas and D. Olkowski (eds.), *Gilles Deleuze and the theatre of philosophy*, London: Routledge.

Butler, J. (2005) *Giving an account of oneself*, New York: Fordham University Press.

Cixous, H. (1993) *Three steps on the ladder of writing* (trans. Sarah Cornell and Susan Sellers), New York: Columbia University Press.

Clough, P. T. (2007) 'Introduction,' in P. T. Clough (ed.), *The affective turn: Theorizing the social*, Durham: Duke University Press. 1–33.

Clough, P. T. (2008) '(De)coding the subject-in-affect,' *Subjectivity*, 23(1). 140–155.

Colebrook, C. (2002) *Gilles Deleuze*, London: Routledge.

Davies, B. (1992) Women's subjectivity and feminist stories,' in C. Ellis and M. Flaherty (eds.), *Investigating subjectivity: research on lived experience*, Newbury Park, CA: Sage. 53–76.

Davies, B. (1994) *Poststructuralist theory and classroom practice*, Geelong: Deakin University Press.

Davies, B. (2000a) *(In)scribing body/landscape relations*, Walnut Creek, CA: AltaMira Press.

Davies, B. (2000b) *A body of writing 1989–1999*, Walnut Creek, CA: AltaMira Press.

Davies, B. (2009) 'Foreword,' in Gale, K. and Wyatt, J. (2009) *Between the two. A nomadic inquiry into collaborative writing and subjectivity*, Newcastle upon Tyne: Cambridge Scholars Publishing.

Davies, B. (2010a) 'The struggle between the individualised subject of phenomenology and the multiplicities of the poststructuralist subject: the problem of agency,' *Reconceptualizing Educational Research Methodology*, 1(1). 54–68.

Davies, B. (2010b) 'Open listening: creative evolution in early childhood settings,' Keynote address presented to the *OMEP: World Organization for Early Childhood Education XXVI World Congress*, Gothenburg, Sweden, August 2010.

Davies, B. and Davies, C. (2007) 'Having or being had by experience,' *Qualitative Inquiry*, 13(8). 1139–1159.

Davies, B., Dormer, S., Gannon, S., Laws, C., Rocco, S., Lenz Taguchi, H. and McCann, H. (2001) 'Becoming schoolgirls: the ambivalent project of subjectification,' *Gender and Education*, 13(2). 167–182.

Davies, B. and Gannon, S. (2006) *Doing collective biography*, Maidenhead: Open University Press.

Davies, B. and Gannon, S. (2009) *Pedagogical encounters*, New York: Peter Lang.

Deleuze, G. (1973) *Proust and signs* (trans. R. Howard), London: Allen Lane/Penguin.

Deleuze, G. (1980) 'Cours Vincennes 12/21/1980,' Available HTTP: <http://www.web-deleuze.com/php/texte.php?cle=190andgroupe=Spinoza andlangue=2)> (accessed 10 February 2010).

Deleuze, G. (1994) *Difference and repetition* (trans. Paul Patton), New York: Columbia University Press.

Deleuze, G. (1995) *Negotiations 1972–1990* (trans. Martin Joughin), New York: Columbia University Press.

Deleuze, G. (1998) *Gilles Deleuze: Essays critical and clinical* (trans. Daniel Smith and Michael Greco), London: Verso.

Deleuze, G. (2004a) *Desert islands and other texts 1953–1974*, New York: Semiotext(e).

Deleuze, G. (2004b) *Francis Bacon: The logic of sensation*, London: Continuum.

Deleuze, G. (2004c) *The logic of sense*, London: Continuum.

Deleuze, G. (2007) *Two regimes of madness: Texts and interviews 1975–1995*, New York: Semiotext(e).

Deleuze, G. and Guattari, F. (2004a) *Anti Oedipus. Capitalism and schizophrenia* (trans. Robert Hurley, Mark Seem, and Helen R. Lane), London: Continuum.

Deleuze, G., and Guattari, F. (2004b) *A thousand plateaus* (Trans. Brian Massumi), London: Continuum.

Deleuze, G. and Parnet, C. (2002) *Dialogues II* (Trans. Hugh Tomlinson and Barbara Habberjam), London: Continuum.

Dell, M. and Whybrow, M. (2003) *Virginia Woolf and Vanessa Bell. Remembering St Ives*, Padstow: Tabb House.

Ellis, C. (2004) *The ethnographic I: A methodological novel about autoethnography*, Walnut Creek: AltaMira Press.

Foucault, M. (1975) *I, Pierre Rivere, Having slaughtered my mother, my sister and my brother: A case of parricide in nineteenth century* (trans. F. Jellinek), Harmondworth: Penguin.

Foucault, M. (2000) 'An interview with Michel Foucault,' in J. Faubion (ed.), *Essential works of Foucault 1954–1984, Volume 3, Michel Foucault: Power*, New York: The New Press (Original interview conducted 1980). 239–297.

Foucault, M. (1977) Discipline & Punish:The Birth of the Prison. Trans. ALan Sheridan. New York: Vintage Press.

Friedan, B. (1963) *The feminine mystique*, New York: W.W. Norton

Gale, K., Pelias, R., Russell, L., Spry, T., and Wyatt, J. (2008) 'Five ways of caring: The complexity of a loving performance,' *4th International Congress of Qualitative Inquiry*. University of Illinois, Urbana-Champaign, May.

Gale, K., Pelias, R., Russell, L., Spry, T., and Wyatt, J. (2009) 'Becoming Encumbered: Variations on a Theme of Intensity,' *5th International Congress of Qualitative Inquiry*. University of Illinois, Urbana-Champaign, May.

Gale, K., Speedy, J. and Wyatt, J. (2010) 'Gatecrashing the oasis? A joint dissertation play,' *Qualitative Inquiry*, 16 (1). 21–28.

Gale, K. and Wyatt, J. (2006) 'Inquiring into writing: An interactive interview,' *Qualitative Inquiry*, 12(6). 1117–1134.

Gale, K. and Wyatt, J. (2007) 'Two men talking,' 3rd *International Congress of Qualitative Inquiry*, University of Illinois, Urbana-Champaign, May.

Gale, K. and Wyatt, J. (2008a) *'Two men talking two: Therapy—A story,'* 4th *International Congress of Qualitative Inquiry*, University of Illinois, Urbana-Champaign, May.

Gale, K. and Wyatt, J. (2008b) 'Becoming men, becoming-men? A collective biography,' *International Review of Qualitative Research*, 1(2). 235–254.

Gale K. and Wyatt J. (2008c) *Between the two: a nomadic inquiry into collaborative writing and subjectivity*, unpublished doctoral thesis, University of Bristol.

Gale, K. and Wyatt, J. (2009) *Between the Two. A nomadic inquiry into collaborative writing and subjectivity*, Newcastle upon Tyne: Cambridge Scholars Publishing.

Gannon, S. (2004) 'Crossing "Boundaries" with the collective girl: A poetic intervention into sex education,' *Sex Education*, 4(1). 81–99.

Gannon, S. (2006) 'The (im)possibilities of writing the self: French Poststructural theory and autoethnography,' *Cultural Studies* ↔ *Critical Methodologies*, 6(4). 474–495.

Hallward, P. (2002) 'Translator's introduction,' in Badiou, A. *Ethics. An essay on the understanding of evil*, London: Verso. vii–xlvii.

Halsey, M. (2007) 'Molar ecology: what can the (full) body of an eco-tourist do?,' in A. Hickey-Moody and P. Malins (eds.) *Deleuzian encounters. Studies in contemporary social issues*, Houndmills: Palgrave Macmillan. 135–150.

Haug, F. et al. (1987) *Female sexualisation*, London: Verso.

Hofmann, M. (1999) 'An interview with Michael Hofmann,' Thumbscrew. 13. Available: HTTP: <http://www.poetrymagazines.org.uk/magazine/record.asp?id=8095> (accessed 10 February 2009).

Madison, S. D. (2010) *Acts of activism: Human rights as radical performance*, New York: Cambridge University Press.

Massey, D. (2005) *For space*, London: Sage Publications.

Massumi, B. (2004) 'Translator's foreword: pleasures of philosophy,' in Deleuze, G. and Guattari, F. (2004b) *A thousand plateaus* (trans. Brian Massumi), London: Continuum. ix–xv.

Nancy, J-L. (2007a) *Listening* (trans. Charlotte Mandell), New York: Fordham University Press.

Nancy, J-L. (2007b) *The creation of the world or globalization* (trans. François Raffoul and David Pettigrew), Albany: State University of New York Press.

Pearson, K. A. (1999) *Germinal life: The difference and repetition of Gilles Deleuze*, New York: Routledge.

Peppiatt, M. (2008) *Francis Bacon: Anatomy of an enigma*, London: Constable.

Plant, S. (1999) *Writing on drugs*, London: Faber and Faber.

Readings, B. (1996) *The university in ruins*, Cambridge, MA: Harvard University Press.

Richardson, L. (1997) 'Poetic representation,' in J. Flood, S. Brice Heath and D. Lapp (eds.), *Handbook of research for literacy educators through communicative and visual arts*, New York: Simon and Schuster. 232–238.

Richardson, L. (2000) 'Skirting a pleated text: De-disciplining an academic life,' in E. A. St. Pierre and W. S. Pillow (eds.), *Working the ruins: Feminist poststructural theory and methods in education*, London: Routledge. 153–163.

Richardson, L. and St. Pierre, E. (2005) 'Writing: A method of inquiry,' in N. Denzin and Y. Lincoln (eds.), *Handbook of qualitative research (3rd ed.)*, London: Sage. 959–978.

Slick, G. (1966) (Writer) *White rabbit*, R. Jarrard (Producer). Nashville: RCA Victor.

Stivale, C. (1998) *Gilles Deleuze's ABCs: The folds of friendship*, Baltimore: Johns Hopkins University Press.

Stivale, C. (2000) 'Overview of film: "L'Abécédaire de Gilles Deleuze" with Claire Parnet directed by Pierre-André Boutang' (1996). Available HTTP: <http://www.langlab.wayne.edu/CStivale/D-G/ABCs.html> (accessed 10 February 2009).

St. Pierre, E. A. (1997) 'Circling the text: nomadic writing practices,' *Qualitative Inquiry*, 3(4). 403–417.

White, M. (2000) *Reflections on narrative practice: Essays and interviews*, Adelaide: Dulwich Centre Publications.

Williams, J. (2003) *Gilles Deleuze's difference and repetition*, Edinburgh: Edinburgh University Press.

Wilson, E. A. (2004) *Psychosomatic: Feminism and the neurological body*, Durham: Duke University Press.

Woolf, V. (1992) *To the lighthouse*, London: Penguin.

Wyatt, J., Gale, K., Gannon, S. and Davies, B. (2010) 'Deleuzian Thought and Collaborative Writing: A Play in Four Acts,' *Qualitative Inquiry*, 16(9). 1–13.

Index

About the Authors

Jonathan Wyatt, Ed.D., is the head of professional development at the Oxford Learning Institute, a research fellow at the Department of Education, University of Oxford, and a counselor in primary care within the National Health Service. He is interested in the performative and collaborative writing and autoethnography of life and loss.

Ken Gale, Ed.D., is a lecturer in education working in the Faculty of Education at the University of Plymouth in the United Kingdom. His particular teaching interests are located within the philosophy of education, poststructural theory, and the application of narrative and autoethnographic approaches in education research. His research interests focus on the theory and practice of collaborative and performative writing practices as methods of inquiry and how these might be applied to areas of subjectivity, friendship, gender studies, and in education studies and professional development.

Susanne Gannon, Ph.D., is an associate professor in the School of Education at the University of Western Sydney, Australia. Much of her work demonstrates her continuing interest in tracing the impact and effects of poststructural theories on writing practices.

Bronwyn Davies, Ph.D., is an independent scholar based in Sydney, Australia. She is also a professorial fellow at the University of Melbourne. The distinctive features of her work are her development of innovative social science research methodologies incorporating elements of the visual, literary, and performative arts on the one hand and its strong base in the conceptual work of poststructuralist philosophers such as Butler, Deleuze, and Foucault on the other.

OMPLICATED

CONVERSATION

A BOOK SERIES OF CURRICULUM STUDIES

This series employs research completed in various disciplines to construct textbooks that will enable public school teachers to reoccupy a vacated public domain—not simply as "consumers" of knowledge, but as active participants in a "complicated conversation" that they themselves will lead. In drawing promiscuously but critically from various academic disciplines and from popular culture, this series will attempt to create a conceptual montage for the teacher who understands that positionality as aspiring to reconstruct a "public" space. *Complicated Conversation* works to resuscitate the progressive project—an educational project in which self-realization and democratization are inevitably intertwined; its task as the new century begins is nothing less than the intellectual formation of a public sphere in education.

The series editor is:

> Dr. William F. Pinar
> Department of Curriculum Studies
> 2125 Main Mall
> Faculty of Education
> University of British Columbia
> Vancouver, British Columbia V6T 1Z4
> CANADA

To order other books in this series, please contact our Customer Service Department:

> (800) 770-LANG (within the U.S.)
> (212) 647-7706 (outside the U.S.)
> (212) 647-7707 FAX

Or browse online by series:

> www.peterlang.com